Whistle in the Piney Woods

Paul Bremond and the Houston, East and West Texas Railway

Whistle in the Piney Woods

Paul Bremond and the Houston, East and West Texas Railway

By

Robert S. Maxwell

Introduction by

Archie P. McDonald

East Texas Historical Association
and
University of North Texas Press
Denton, Texas

First edition Texas Gulf Coast Historical Association Publication Series
Volume VII, Number 2, November 1963
Granted the L. R. Bryan, Jr. Award for 1963

5 4 3 2 1

The paper used in this book meets the minimum requirements of the American National Standard for Permanence of Paper for Printed Library Materials, z39.48.1984. Binding materials have been chosen for durability.

Library of Congress Cataloging-in-Publication Data

Maxwell, Robert S.
Whistle in the Piney Woods : Paul Bremond and the Houston, East and West Texas Railway / by Robert S. Maxwell. —1st ed.
p. cm.
Originally published: Houston? : Texas Gulf Coast Historical Association, 1963, in series: Texas Gulf Coast Historical Association. Publication series ; v. 7, no. 2. With new introd.
Includes bibliographical references and index.
ISBN 1-57441-061-X (alk. paper)
1. Houston, East and West Texas Railway Company. 2. Railroads—Texas, East—History. 3. Logging railroads—Texas, East—History. 4. Bremond, Paul, 1810–1885. 5. Texas, East—History. I. Title.
TF25.H68M39 1998
384.5'4'09764—dc21 98-33659
CIP

Design by Accent Design and Communications

To Roger Montgomery and
Charlotte Baker Montgomery
“Whose father listened for the first
Whistle in the Piney Woods.”

Contents

Acknowledgments ix

Introduction xi

I • Mr. Bremond 1

II • Opening the Piney Woods 11

III • Completion and Receivership 27

IV • Financial Structure, Organization, and Operations 39

V • Reorganization and Consolidation 60

VI • Connecting Lines 71

VII • "The Rabbit" 94

Notes 103

Bibliography 114

Index 119

Acknowledgments

Many people have contributed to the writing and production of this study of the pioneer railroad in the Piney Woods. The administration at Stephen F. Austin State College has shown both interest and encouragement in the project and through the Bureau of East Texas Research has provided me with time and travel funds to pursue the story. The officials of the Southern Pacific Lines have extended every courtesy and have opened their files and private records without restriction for my perusal. Mr. F. I. Tucker, of Nacogdoches, has kindly read the manuscript and made a number of helpful suggestions. Several persons, including my wife, Margaret Dunning Maxwell, have assisted in typing and editing the copy. The Texas Gulf Coast Historical Association is to be thanked for providing for the publication of the work, as is editor James A. Tinsley for his patience and care in preparing the manuscript for the printer. The errors, of course, are all my own.

Robert S. Maxwell,
Stephen F. Austin State College
Nacogdoches, Texas
October 1, 1963

Introduction

In October 1997, the East Texas Historical Association, the Texas Folklore Society, and the Pineywoods Foundation produced "Whistle In The Piney Woods: A Symposium On Railroads And Logging In East Texas." The inspiration for the symposium came from Robert S. Maxwell's book with nearly the same title published by the Texas Gulf Coast Historical Association in 1963.

Bob Maxwell was born in Newport, Kentucky. He played and coached basketball and remained all his life a sports enthusiast, though in time his participation settled on golf. Maxwell served in the army during WWII as a company commander. He received academic degrees from Kentucky Wesleyan, the University of Cincinnati, and the University of Wisconsin, and taught at the universities of Wisconsin and Kentucky before moving to Stephen F. Austin State University. Up there, he had earned a national reputation in the history of the Progressive Era; in East Texas, he became *the* authority on the history of forests and railroads.

Bob was named a Distinguished Professor and the first Regent's Professor at Stephen F. Austin State University. He was a Fulbright lecturer at Southampton in England, chaired the Department of History at Stephen F. Austin State University, served as a director of the national Forest History Society, faithfully attended Kiwanis meetings, and was a mainstay of Christ Episcopal Church. And he and Mrs. Maxwell—Margaret Dunning Maxwell—traveled the world.

Maxwell's *Sawdust Empire*, written with Bob Baker, was the first and remains the definitive work on Texas forest history. It was based on resources in the Forest History Collection in the Ralph W. Steen Library at Stephen F. Austin State University, a collection that owes its origin to Robert Maxwell. Even earlier, Maxwell had established himself as an authority on Texas railroads—especially their symbiotic relationship with forests and the lumber industry—with the publication of *Whistle In The Piney Woods.* This is a history of the Houston, East and West Texas Railroad, its founder Paul Bremond, and its role in the development of East Texas.

Copies of *Whistle In The Piney Woods* were so rare that when we planned the symposium we had to work from a xerox copy supplied by Carol Riggs, director of the Texas Forestry Museum, who confessed that she had gotten her copy from the Kurth Library in Lufkin. Even before the symposium was held on October 18, 1997, we had decided to republish this rare, and more importantly, crucial book on the development of an East Texas industry. Permission to do so was granted by Mrs. Maxwell and by James Tinsley, representing the Texas Gulf Coast Historical Association.

Fran Vick, director of the University of North Texas Press, contributed her expertise in book production and distribution. F. E. Abernethy, my mentor and collaborator on the symposium, selected the illustrations and assisted with proofreading and other necessaries for such a project. Mrs. Portia Gordon worked the magic of scanning the original text to a disk. Hardy Meredith made reproducible copies of the illustrations Ab located in the archives, another form of magic. The Pineywoods Foundation, the East Texas Historical Association, and the University of North Texas Press found the funds to complete the project. And I got out of the way and watched in wonder as these experts applied their skills to make this classic book on East Texas available to a modern audience.

This edition contains more illustrations and may be bound more handsomely, but the work is substantially as Maxwell published it a third of a century ago. We have corrected some typographical blunders, and perhaps made a few of our own in the process. We hope that a new generation will profit from this "'Whistle In The Piney Woods' that signaled progress and civilization to the East Texas region."

Archie P. McDonald
Director, East Texas Historical Association

Paul Bremond
courtesy Bob Bowman

I

Mr. Bremond

This is the story of a railroad and the dreams and schemes of the man who built it.

In 1875, when the history of the Houston, East and West Texas Railway begins, there were less than seventy-five thousand miles of railroad in the entire United States. During the pioneer period, beginning with the first fledgling lines in Maryland and South Carolina in 1830, railroad building was a highly individualistic and often personal enterprise. Most were unrelated short lines connecting two relatively isolated towns or cities and usually built with local funds. Though hundreds of charters were issued, only a small number of the early companies succeeded in building railroads and even fewer survived the initial years. They exhibited a great variety of locomotives, cars, gauges, track, road beds, and equipment. For example, rails ranged from wood, to iron straps, to steel. Railroad gauges varied from three to six feet. A passenger could expect to change trains perhaps a half-dozen times in a fifty mile trip.[1]

The movement to consolidate these numerous short lines into larger systems began as early as the 1850s and, despite the Civil War, by 1875 the pattern of these mergers and consolidations was apparent throughout the country. In addition to combining ownership, consolidated lines standardized the gauge, the size and weight of rails, rolling stock, and service. The resulting railroad was a much more valuable property than the sum of the independent short lines and could perform much more work. This development of the large systems and the continuing boom in railroad construction was accompanied by the rise of great railroad tycoons. These financial and industrial giants boldly blue-printed the further development of America's rail network, and, in many cases, at the same time so manipulated their holdings to amass great fortunes for themselves. The Vanderbilts with the New York Central System, Jay Gould with the Missouri Pacific and related roads, James J. Hill and the Great Northern, and the "Big Four," Collis P. Huntington, Leland Stanford, Mark Hopkins, and Charles Crocker, with the Southern Pacific system, are well-known examples of this trend. Altogether, in the two-and-a-half decades from 1875 to 1900, American railroad builders constructed more than 100,000 miles of track, an amount almost equal to the construction totals of all other years in the United States combined.[2]

But not all of the railroads were built by great tycoons. In fact, local persons of limited means and experience constructed more than one-half of the track laid down during these years. Small independent companies, without significant financial resources and without affiliation with the large trunk lines, frequently sought to build into isolated, rural areas, to open new sections to commercial opportunity, and to link inland towns with the larger port cities. The fact that these local short lines often failed, were forced into receivership, or were either abandoned or taken over by some larger system did not prevent new groups from securing charters almost every year to build a railroad which they were certain would open up a new region and incidentally make their own fortunes. Very often such enterprises were dominated by a single individual. He would pour his time, energy, and personal resources into the project and frequently carry it to conclusion despite setbacks, failures, and discouragements. Such a man was Paul Bremond, who built the Houston, East and West Texas Railway through the Piney Woods of East Texas and opened that region to the outside world. The man and his railroad provide a significant case study of the development of short lines in the United States. The story is a worthy addition to the history of American railroads as well as to the history of the East Texas region.

The beginning of railroad building in Texas came, as might be expected, some two decades after the first roads were constructed in the East. Although several charters were issued during the period of the Republic, none of the companies succeeded in building a railroad, and it was not until 1853 that the Buffalo Bayou, Brazos & Colorado Railway announced a regular schedule from Harrisburg (now absorbed by Houston) to Stafford's Point, a distance of twenty miles. This was followed by the Houston and Texas Central (originally the Galveston and Red River), the Galveston, Houston and Henderson, the Houston Tap and Brazoria, and the Texas and New Orleans, all radiating from the Houston area and connecting with the rich agriculture lands in the surrounding counties and with the port of Galveston. Altogether some eleven railroads were built and in operation prior to 1861, having a total trackage of 468 miles.[3]

The Civil War brought an actual decline in railroad mileage in Texas. Many companies defaulted and ceased operations. Others were cannibalized. The years immediately after the war witnessed a slow and difficult recovery, but some consolidation and planning had given a greater sense of purpose to the several short lines. By 1875 there were still only 1600 miles of railroad in Texas, but the vision of a transcontinental system and connections with the metropolitan centers of the East would soon explode in a boom in railroad building. The Texas and Pacific had reached Dallas from Shreveport, and a northern branch stretched from Texarkana to Sherman. The International and Great Northern ran from Austin to Longview with a branch from Houston joining the main line at Palestine. The Texas and New Orleans skirted the Gulf Coast east of Houston to the Sabine River on its way to New Orleans. A trunk line, the Galveston, Houston and Henderson, connected the port city of Galveston with Houston. The Galveston, Harrisburg and San Antonio inched westward toward the old Spanish capital, and the Houston and Texas Central stretched through the rich blacklands north to Dallas. And that was all.

Significantly, these rails did no more than skirt the edges of the East Texas pine belt. This great region, comprising more than twelve million acres of valuable timber land, lay largely between the T&P tracks on the north and the T&NO route on the south, the I&GN on the west, and the Texas-Louisiana boundary on the east. Despite the growing demands for lumber on the plains and the increasing market for manufactured goods in the East Texas region, transportation remained slow, arduous, and costly. The heart of the Piney Woods was yet to be tapped by the railroads. The Sabine, Neches, and Trinity rivers were used at times to ship goods northward by steamboat and to float logs downstream to Beaumont, Orange, and Galveston. But the level of water was very unpredictable, navigation was treacherous, and hundreds of logs were lost, to further congest the rivers.

Overland, wagons pulled by teams of mules and oxen transported lumber, cotton, and other articles for hundreds of miles to the coast or rail outlets, thus increasing the cost of such items 600 to 700 percent. The towns were small, straggling, and isolated, and the people were insular, largely uneducated, and suspicious of outsiders. The roads were poor, ranging from merely rough to impassable. It took the mail two days to reach

Nacogdoches from Crockett, the nearest railhead on the I&GN, a distance of sixty-five miles.[4] Yet, if this region could be opened by adequate rail transportation, its natural resources could be exploited with beneficial results for all.

Numerous plans had been made to tap this region, and several railroad charters had been secured. The Galveston and Red River Railroad had been chartered in 1848 with plans to cross the western edge of the pineries. The Galveston, Houston and Henderson Railroad Company was chartered in 1853 to go directly through the Piney Woods. The Eastern Texas Railroad Company was the successor to the Mexican, Henderson and Gulf which in turn succeeded the Henderson and Burkville, neither of which actually constructed any track. The Eastern Texas, chartered in 1858, proposed to run from Sabine Pass, via Beaumont and Nacogdoches, through the pine lands to Henderson. It was completed between the Pass and Beaumont, and construction was continuing north in 1861 when the Civil War brought an end to railroad building. During the war the rolling stock was moved on the T&NO to Houston and part of the rails were taken up and used for the construction of forts. Thus, all the schemes had failed or were diverted, and East Texas still was without rail connections. It remained for Paul Bremond to translate the dream into reality.[5]

Bremond was, in truth, a unique individual. He was a man of many enterprises, a bold entrepreneur in the true American spirit, and a man of great personal magnetism. He was born in New York City, October 11, 1810. His father was Dr. Paul Barlie Bremond, who had emigrated from France in 1805, and his mother was an American girl, Catherine Green Bremond, of Fishkill, New York. Young Paul left school at the age of twelve and was apprenticed to a firm of hatters. When he was nineteen, Bremond and a friend opened a small hat store in the Bowery. Paul worked at the bench making and finishing hats while his partner conducted the store. Unfortunately, too much of the business was done on credit, and bad debts swallowed the earnings. The partnership was dissolved, and Bremond, age twenty, moved to Philadelphia. There he persuaded a friend to finance him in a small hat-making shop where he received hats in the rough and finished and sold them himself. The business prospered, and at the end of six years it is said that he had accumulated some $40,000. Most of this, however, he lost in the panic of 1837. He determined, in 1839, to move to Galveston and engage in business there.

Galveston at this time was a city of more than 3,000 people, the chief port of entry, and the principal city of the Republic of Texas. So, with his wife and two small children, Bremond embarked for Texas on the schooner *W. I. Watson* and had his merchandise and household belongings shipped on the brig *Virginia*. The brig, however, was wrecked while trying to negotiate the north breaker of the island, and all of his belongings were lost, leaving young Bremond practically bankrupt.

Fortunately, the city auctioneer, John Sydnor, assisted him in opening a small store near the old customs house. The next year he opened his own auction and commission business. About 1842, he moved to Houston and operated a general merchandise and commission business there. He prospered and soon extended his interests to other ventures, associating himself with William A. Van Alstyne, William Marsh Rice, and other rising Houston businessmen.

Bremond was particularly interested in transportation. He had been one of the original incorporators of the Galveston and Red River Railroad and in 1850 became a leading stockholder in the Brazos Plank Road project which sought to build a plank road from Houston to tap the rich cotton country of the Brazos valley. Despite this interest Bremond continued to push for a railroad to be built from Houston to central Texas, and urged that investments in the plank road not be allowed to stand in the way of the larger project. As a result the Galveston and Red River railroad was reactivated with Bremond as the chief promoter. Associated with him were Rice, Van Alstyne, Ebenezer Allen, B. A. Shepherd, Dr. Francis Moore, James H. Stevens, W. J. Hutchins, T. W. House, and others.

Ground was broken in 1855 and the road was pushed northward rapidly, reaching Cypress the next year and Hempstead in 1858. The name of the railroad was changed to the Houston and Texas Central, and the road eventually was completed to Navasota, Corsicana, and Dallas. Bremond remained president of the H&TC until 1858, when he relinquished control to Abraham Groesbeck. The H&TC went through receivership and eventual reorganization but Bremond continued to have a heavy investment in this road until about 1875.[6]

Many stories were told of Bremond and his methods of operation. Most illustrate his bulldog determination and his earnest belief in himself. Once, while he was building the H&TC, he had a small army of Irishmen working for him as section hands. The company ran short of funds and fell behind some three months in the payroll. The men finally determined to take matters in their own hands and have a showdown with the boss. They marched on Bremond's home, a large white frame house located on Capitol Avenue in Houston, with threatening gestures and a variety of improvised weapons. After milling around for a while, they tore down the fence surrounding the house and threatened to ransack his home. At this point, Bremond braved the mob and came out to talk with them. A man of phenomenal memory, he was said to have known all of his workers by sight and name. This facility he developed not because of any feeling of "democracy" or "mixing qualities" but as a measure of self-protection. Before he was through he had convinced them that their best chance to get paid was to stick by him. He promised that eventually they would receive every cent that they were due. So persuasive was he that the leaders expressed regret for the trouble they had caused and promised to rebuild his fence. On another occasion a sub-contractor despaired of payment for his work and took his case to an attorney. The lawyer agreed to represent him but wanted to bring the contractor and Bremond together for a conference in hopes that the controversy could be settled amicably. This the outraged contractor refused to do, explaining that if they let Bremond talk, he would convince the lawyer that the contractor owed Bremond money. Nevertheless the attorney went to Bremond to discuss the case. Sure enough, when he returned the attorney told his client, "I think you have treated Bremond damned shabbily. I'll have nothing to do with your case."[7]

It was said that Bremond was a near-magician in financing speculative ventures. With scarcely enough money to build ten miles of railroad he had built more than fifty miles of good road on the H&TC, using promises for currency, promises enough to have reached the North Pole. Yet, when the road reached the rich blacklands and began a lucrative business, Bremond's first care was to fulfill the promises that he had made. It was said that no man who trusted Paul Bremond, willingly or unwillingly as did the Irish workers, ever lost a cent by doing so.

Bremond was a strong family man and he raised a large family. When he was only twenty-one, he married Harriet Martha Sprouls of New York. Of this union there were three children: one son, Edward L., and two daughters, Margaret and Harriet. Edward was associated with his father in his railroad ventures and at one time was Fire Chief of Houston. Margaret Bremond was the first wife of William Marsh Rice, capitalist and benefactor of Rice University. Harriet Bremond married Samuel Coulter Timpson and after his death in 1882 married James Appleby. After the death of Harriet Sprouls Bremond in 1846, Bremond married Mary E. Van Alstyne, daughter of William A. Van Alstyne, a prominent businessman in Houston and one of Bremond's partners. This marriage produced five daughters of whom four grew to maturity. Pauline married John A. Dozier, Kate married J. C. Zimmer, Julia married Lucas Fernandez, and Nettie married Walter Lufkin. Timpson, Appleby, and Dozier, and perhaps Lufkin and Zimmer, were associated with Bremond in his business ventures. Mary Van Alstyne Bremond died in 1884, and in 1870 Bremond was married for the third time, this time to the American-born Viscountess de Valernes, known in family circles as Mary Louise. There were no children by this marriage.

Though his first two wives and the children were devout Episcopalians, Paul Bremond himself was an earnest believer in spiritualism. Under his leadership a small society of students of spiritualism was formed in Houston and held regular meetings, frequently attended by some visiting practitioner from the East. Bremond made frequent trips to New York to attend spiritualist conferences and was much interested in the then popular theory of "Spiritual Photography." He believed that his personal contact and spirit guide was Moseley Baker, a soldier of the Texas Revolution and a veteran of the battle of San Jacinto. He credited Baker with giving him the advice to build the H&TC and later claimed that the spirit prompted him to build a second road. According to Bremond, when five years went by without action, the spirit of Baker became insistent and urged him to "proceed with the work."[8]

Paul Bremond admittedly had his idiosyncrasies. His self-confidence, his persuasive manner, his air of command, and his interest in spiritualism set him apart from his neighbors. He was not always a popular man because his aloofness and reserve, as well as his business drive, made some very bitter enemies. But Bremond was a builder and had the confidence of his own soul. At the time of our narrative (1875), he was a plump, bright-eyed, old-fashioned gentleman of sixty-five, with white hair and beard. He always wore a stock instead of a tie and affected clothes with an Eastern cut. Though not tall, he was an arresting figure and gave the impression that he could command millions. It became his dream to build a railroad through the Piney Woods.[9]

HE&WT narrow gauge engine (?) number 17
courtesy James T. Vogler and Harry J. Heaney

II

Opening the Piney Woods

Although the Houston and Texas Central was a broad-gauge road, Bremond became a convert after the war to the superiority of the narrow three-foot gauge. This belief was strengthened when he visited Philadelphia in 1875 and viewed the operation of a narrow-gauge road on the grounds of the Centennial Exposition. Bremond was certain that a narrow gauge would be quicker to build, cheaper to maintain and equip, and equally efficient as the broad gauge for the relatively short hauls and local traffic that would be characteristic of an East Texas railroad. So, the Houston East and West Texas Railway was to be narrow gauge.[1]

The state legislature approved the charter of the HE&WT under its general laws in routine fashion on March 11, 1875. It was quite broad and generous. The charter provided for capital stock not to exceed $10,000,000 which was to be divided into shares of $100 each. Each share entitled its owner to one vote and the company could do business after the first $100,000 had been paid in. The legislature authorized the company to build to Texarkana on the Red River, with branches to the Sabine through Jasper and/or Shelby Counties, a branch to Tyler and Waco, and a western line to

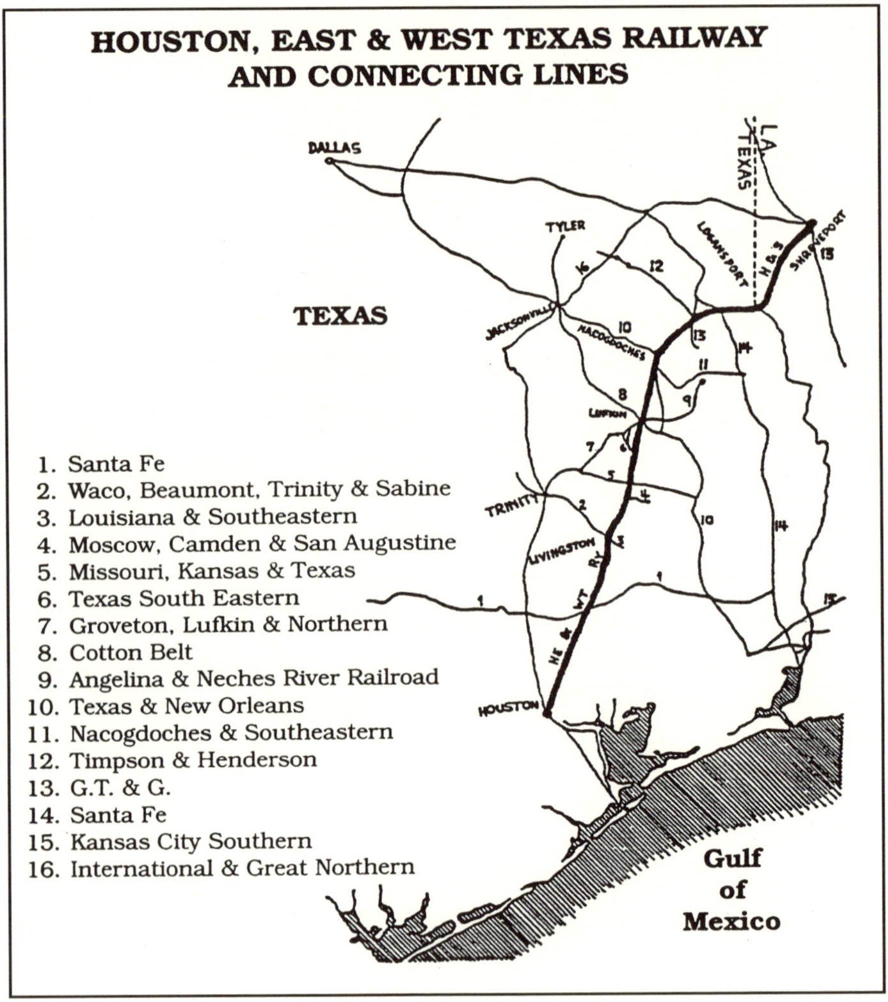

Corpus Christi and Laredo. The charter required that at least twenty miles of track be built within two years and at least twenty more each year until completion. It authorized the company to condemn land and approved a state land grant of sixteen sections of land per mile after it had constructed an initial ten miles of track.

The company held its first meeting in Houston on April 7, 1875. In addition to Bremond, the minutes listed W. D. Cleveland, Peter Floeck, John Shearn, F. A. Rice, Henry Fox, W. J. Hutchins, Abraham Groesbeck, S. C. Timpson, T. W. House, Ben A. Botts, E. W. Cave, Eugene Pillot, J. S. Roberts, and J. T. Brady as the original incorporators and named Bremond, Rice, Timpson, Fox, Cleveland, Groesbeck, and Shearn as directors. At the initial meeting of stockholders Paul Bremond held 1000 shares of capital stock, and all of the other incorporators apparently held one share each. Bremond was elected president and Shearn secretary.[2]

The *Houston Telegraph* welcomed the venture with the announcement that "another narrow gauge railroad" was to be built in the immediate future. The road would run northeast and would tap a rich timber country which in turn would enrich Houston. The paper predicted that soon Houston would have 100,000 people and would be the rail center of Texas.[3]

Construction, however, did not get underway until July of the next year. The *Telegraph* reported the ceremonies (perhaps on Independence Day) in which Bremond threw up the first spade of earth at a point near the old T&NO station. Here, in a brief speech, Bremond urged that this new rail line be locally owned and controlled. He cited the experience of the H&TC Railway and implored his listeners to invest in the new venture.[4] Following these formalities, Colonel Frank Noble put his crews to work laying track along the route north and east of town surveyed by W. E. Woods.[5]

The work force was recruited wherever they could be found. Local Negroes, recent immigrants from Galveston, farmers who would hire out with their teams by the day, and more experienced section hands from other roads all went to work for Woods and Noble. Lightweight rails resting on rough green ties stretched across the flats in the fringe of the Piney Woods. At the west fork of the San Jacinto River, Noble conquered his first major obstacle. The lesser streams had been crossed by means of green pine trestles, cut from the forest in the vicinity of the crossing and dragged to the bank by mule or oxen teams. But this crossing demanded a center pier and iron or steel construction. The bridge, purchased from the Cincinnati Bridge Company, was transported down the Mississippi River by barge and hence around to Houston by ship. When in place, the San Jacinto bridge made an impressive sight. For this bridge, Bremond paid the Cincinnati company the magnificent sum of $7000.[6] Once across, the road was built rapidly to the station of New Caney. By April of 1877 Bremond could report that twenty miles of the HE&WT were completed.[7]

The motive power for the fledgling railroad was furnished by two narrow gauge locomotives with interesting histories. While at the Philadelphia Centennial Exposition, Bremond had admired the two gaily painted engines which were used to haul passengers and commodities around the grounds. Bremond purchased the locomotives for delivery after the exposition closed. Consequently, in the fall of 1876, the "Girard" and the "Centennial" began their long journey by ship down the Delaware River, around the coast to the Gulf and then to Galveston. There Charles A. Burton, machinist and engineer who had been with Bremond since H&TC days, supervised the unloading and assembly of the pert puffer bellies. Their cost was listed at $11,501.60.[8]

By the spring of 1878, Bremond was running regular service to New Caney in Montgomery County and by that fall had reached the town of Cleveland, a distance of forty-three miles. The schedule advertised a daily train to New Caney and Cleveland leaving Houston at 9:00 A.M. and returning at 6:00 P.M. At the December stockholders meeting, Bremond announced that the state inspector, Colonel E. F. Gray, had completed his inspection of the required minimum stretch of track and the company was now entitled to receive the first installment of its state land grant, sixteen sections of land for every mile of road built.[9] It was also reported that five sawmills were now operating along the right-of-way with a combined capacity of 100,000 feet of lumber per day.

To increase revenues, Bremond ran frequent excursions. One trip to the San Jacinto Springs became a standard Sunday excursion during the entire spring and summer of 1878. Trains left Houston at 9:00 A.M. and at 2:30 and 4:15 P.M. The round trip fare was fifty cents for adults and a quarter for children. At the springs the passengers were afforded fishing, swimming, boating, picnicking, and dancing. To please the moralists, strict order was maintained and no drinking of spirits was allowed. As an added attraction a band from St. Louis played both in the afternoon and evening. The venture evidently was popular, for the excursions continued until fall.[10]

From Cleveland, the line was steadily stretched northward. The stations of Africa, Round Prairie, Shepherd, Milledge Station, and Urbana were reached by early 1879, and the engineers tackled the formidable task of bridging the Trinity River.[11] In contrast to the San Jacinto River bridge, it was determined to cross the Trinity by means of a trestle. Under the direction of a Major Goodwin, construction crews set to work building a wooden bridge 2300 feet long to span the river above the high water mark. The timbers were cut in the immediate vicinity, partly from the company's own right-of-way, and were dragged to the bridge site by teams of oxen or mules driven by local farmers who hired out by the day with their animals. When this long wooden trestle was completed, it was only a short distance to Goodrich, which the construction crew reached in the early summer of 1879, a distance of sixty-four miles from Houston. In the meantime, surveyor W. E. Wood, with a corps of assistants, ran the prospective line well beyond the Trinity, across Polk County.

Every settlement and village watched anxiously as Wood proceeded to survey, locate and acquire options for the proposed right-of-way.[12]

During this same year (1879), the directors of the road determined to publish a pamphlet called *Prospectus* advertising the East Texas region and the HE&WT in hopes of stimulating the sale of bonds and the purchase of lands adjoining the right-of-way. This pamphlet was published in New York in 1880 and praised the rich opportunities in East Texas opened up by the penetration of the Piney Woods. The road, which was erroneously said to have been begun in 1877, was building through twelve counties containing 150,000 people who produced annually 100,000 bales of cotton. These counties held more than 1,000,000 acres of timber, the *Prospectus* added. It described Bremond as an experienced railroad builder who had been a leader in the construction of the H&TC. He would, said the *Prospectus,* invest $500,000 and three years service in the new project, which then extended to Livingston and was earning more than the interest on its authorized debt per mile. It had nineteen sawmills along its route which produced 200,000 board feet of lumber daily. When the road reached Marshall, continued the *Prospectus,* it would connect with the Texas and Pacific. Plans were also well advanced to build a line west, seventy miles to Waco, and other branches to the Red River and to the Sabine. The total cost of the road, including bridges, was estimated to average between $10,000 and $12,000 per mile. The merits of the narrow-gauge road, as opposed to the broad or standard gauge, were argued convincingly. Narrow gauge was more economical to build and could be operated more cheaply than the broad gauge, the *Prospectus* concluded, as the experience of the Denver and Rio Grande Railway had demonstrated. Finally, a map of the road was attached which showed the HE&WT with a main line extending from Houston to Nacogdoches and Logansport, Louisiana, and branches to Tyler, Texarkana, Waco, and Corpus Christi.[13]

Bremond was anxious that local interests, both in Houston and in the smaller towns along the route, provide the funds for the building of the HE&WT. He hoped that in this way he could not only finance the venture, but would also insure a sense of responsibility and personal interest in the prosperity of the railroad by the people who used it. His experience with the H&TC had convinced him that local financing would be far more flexible and satisfactory than securing the necessary funds in the eastern money markets, doubtless at a high rate of interest. In all of his speeches and letters Bremond stressed the desirability of local financial support for the railroad. It would seem that he largely equated in his mind the degree of local support with the probable success or failure of the venture.[14]

With these arguments in mind Bremond sought to draw into the company many of the principal businessmen of Houston and to persuade them to invest heavily in the venture. But although such men as T. W. House, Abraham Groesbeck, F. A. Rice, and Eugene Pillot lent their names as incorporators and directors of the HE&WT, they evidently held only nominal amounts of stock and did not heavily involve their personal fortunes in the venture. In contrast Bremond staked most of his own resources, estimated at $500,000, and devoted almost all of his time to this enterprise. So thoroughly was the HE&WT identified with the little Frenchman that the press regularly referred to it as "Bremond's Road."[15]

From the ledgers and the journals of the company it would appear that Bremond drew on his own funds and those of the company interchangeably. In addition to specific items for trips to New York, Denver, and Galveston, the entries indicate that he withdrew almost $150,000 while depositing $97,000 in a fifteen-month period in 1881–1882. Beyond this there are minor drafts for advances to members of his family, such as a payment to E. S. Jemison and Co. of New York for a draft of $100 in favor of his daughter, Miss Kate Bremond, who was visiting that city.[16]

Bremond also acquired large quantities of land in his own name, chiefly right-of-ways in the counties through which the road was to run. These he later transferred to the company. This maneuver was probably one of convenience, speed, and economy, so that the price of lands along the route would not unduly rise before the right-of-way was secured. For example, Bremond purchased some 2500 acres from D. W. Heard in Nacogdoches County for the Angelina River crossing site in 1879. In total, not only did he acquire lands in Harris, Montgomery, San Jacinto, Polk, Angelina, Nacogdoches, and Shelby counties (through which the road eventually ran), but also in Tyler, Hardin, Jasper, Hopkins, Wood, and Sabine counties, which were on the route of possible branch lines authorized by the charter. In all, these holdings represented many thousands of acres of land, mostly heavily timbered, which the builder transferred to the HE&WT in 1883. It is apparent that by this time the personal funds of Bremond and his personal holdings were hopelessly enmeshed with those of the company. The HE&WT was very literally "Bremond's Road."[17]

Though Houston financiers and businessmen failed to take more than a nominal interest in the new narrow-gauge venture, Bremond had high hopes that the rural towns could be persuaded to contribute substantially toward the cost of the project. Never far from the surface of the argument was the implied threat that unless the town cooperated, the route of the railroad would be changed to bypass the parsimonius settlement in favor of a more generous rival a few miles away. Usually this threat did not have to be voiced to be effective. The villagers knew only too well the fate of places that were bypassed by the railroads. Yet, Bremond's relations with the rural towns and the counties on the projected route were generally cordial. At a mass meeting in 1876 at Moscow, Polk County, General Agent Horace Cone promised that the railroad would come through the town and praised Bremond's determination to push the project forward as an independent line. The response was immediate. Town lots, county land, forty bales of cotton, and an unspecified amount of cash were subscribed on the spot. After the meeting, according to the press report, the visitors and citizens then "retired to the hotel where all enjoyed a repast amid much hilarity in the club room at the prospect of speedy railroad service."[18]

The next year a similar railroad meeting was held in Livingston on July 4th. After the barbecue celebrating the arrival of the corps of engineers, the leading citizens in turn addressed the crowd explaining the necessity of procuring donations and acquiring right-of-way in order to build from Livingston to Moscow. As a result, five precinct committees were appointed to solicit funds or land from the residents. A central committee supervised the overall direction of the campaign. All were optimistic that Livingston could soon make a most attractive offer to Bremond to insure the coming of the railroad.[19]

In the fall of 1878 the builder organized an excursion on the HE&WT from San Jacinto County to Houston, escorted by his son, E. L. Bremond, Horace Cone, and W. E. Woods. The gentlemen and their ladies were given a quick buffet on their arrival at the depot, and en route back refreshments were served on the cars. During the journey company officials lectured their guests on the advantages of the railroad and the economic boom their city could expect once the railroad had begun regularly scheduled runs. Bremond was praised as an experienced and dedicated builder who was determined to build the road through the Piney Woods. Again the plea was for subscriptions in land, cotton, or money to help finance the construction of the HE&WT. And again, the people responded with some contributions.[20] In like manner, Nacogdoches citizens contributed town lots and right-of-way. They also made up a fund with which to purchase right-of-way property from any obstinate landholder.[21] All looked for great benefits when the railroad arrived.

Despite these and similar efforts to raise funds locally, it soon became apparent that much more money would be needed if the road was to be completed. It was obvious that the local towns were much too poverty stricken and devoid of investment capital to finance any considerable part of a major railroad venture. Accordingly, the directors authorized Bremond to have bonds printed, select a New York bank as trustee, and negotiate the sale of first mortgage bonds to the best interest of the company. Early in 1878 Bremond proceeded to New York to arrange the loan and subsequently executed a twenty-year first-mortgage bond to the Union Trust Company of New York on May 1, 1878. The terms obtained were not attractive because the interest rate was seven percent in contrast to later loans at six percent. In addition, commissions of ten percent were charged, and expenses added still more to the costs. The total amount of first mortgage bonds issued was $1,344,000. Against this was pledged the railroad, its right-of-way, all the rolling stock, track built or to be built, and all stations, terminals, and other buildings.[22] After discounting the commissions, expenses and travel, and the first year's interest, it appears probable that the HE&WT netted about $1,000,000 over a five-year period from this bond issue. This enabled the company to complete the line to Nacogdoches in 1883 and to purchase sufficient rolling stock to operate the road.

In a report to the stockholders in 1880, Bremond announced that the road was going well. It had more than ninety miles of track and could market more bonds. He proposed to send someone to New York to dispose of more bonds and to purchase rails, fasteners, and rolling stock. The directors promptly authorized him to proceed to New York and "take such action as he may deem necessary."[23]

With more money, the HE&WT continued to build northward and reached Livingston in 1879 and Moscow in 1880. The citizens of each town were eager to cooperate and rejoiced that the road would go through their town. At Livingston, the townspeople again welcomed the corps of engineers with a barbecue and organized committees to provide the necessary right-of-way through the county. In Moscow, the arrival of the first train was celebrated with a public dinner.[24] By this time the road had penetrated into the very heart of the Piney Woods and had begun to develop a profitable trade in lumber, cotton, manufactured merchandise, and passenger traffic. The Houston press frequently commented on its activity and noted that "Bremond's Road" was bringing in big trains of lumber every week. During October of 1880 the *Houston Post* quoted railroad officials saying that 376 cars of lumber were brought in that month alone and even more could have been shipped but for the inability of the local lines to transfer the shipments. The HE&WT depot in Houston, valued at $2,000, had been completed and tracks were laid across the city to connect "Bremond's Road" with the Western Narrow Gauge Railroad. In October, 1880, the HE&WT again made news in the *Houston Post* when it brought to town 125 people for the circus; and wonder of wonders, it arrived two hours ahead of schedule![25]

When construction crews reached the Neches River, they bridged it with timbers from the pine forests in the same manner that they had crossed the Trinity. As the road crept northward, new towns sprang up, frequently named for some of the officials of the railroad. Corrigan was named for Pat Corrigan, an official on the first train that reached the town. Fout's Mill (now Wakefield) was so called after the owner of the first saw mill there.

Burke was named after Ed Burke, a civil engineer who supervised the construction of that portion of the line.[26]

From the Neches, the HE&WT ran almost due north through Angelina County. At a point seven miles west of Homer, the county seat, in a clearing in the midst of a dense pine forest, Bremond and the other officials laid out a new town which was to be a major point on the road. It was called Lufkin in honor of Edwin P. Lufkin, chief construction engineer on the HE&WT. Streets were laid out in a neat square plat and the east-west streets were named for officials of the railroad: Burke, Shepherd, Lufkin, Dozier, Groesbeck, Bremond, and Paul.[27] Three years later when the Kansas and Gulf Short Line Railroad (now the Cotton Belt) reached Lufkin from Tyler, there was a great barbecue and land sale which launched the new town into one of the fastest growing cities of the region. It has since become the county seat of Angelina County and one of the principal manufacturing and business centers of East Texas.[28]

Lufkin Depot, painting by R. Ryan
courtesy Claude Smithhart

There is a tradition, well-established in the folklore of Angelina County, that the ancient town of Homer was by-passed because of personal pique. The story holds that the route of the HE&WT was originally surveyed through the old county seat town. There the right-of-way crew celebrated too wildly one Saturday night after payday and as a result landed in the Homer jail. The construction engineer in charge, supposedly Lufkin, was infuriated at the refusal of the local officers to release his men and swore to bypass the town. As a result the road ran seven miles to the west of Homer, a new town was established, the county seat was eventually moved, and Homer died.

This story might well be true. However, the officials of the Southern Pacific Lines are doubtful. Study of the corporation papers in Houston and the Angelina County records indicate that no right-of-way was ever procured to Homer. The map in the *Prospectus,* drawn in 1879, shows the road following its present route through Angelina County. And, equally significant, Bremond acquired the site for the Angelina River crossing in 1879, at a time when the road had not proceeded beyond Goodrich. This site would not have been usable if the road had swung east through Homer. It seems more probable that Paul Bremond, who planned and built the road, never intended to go through Homer. There is no question, however, that the decision to by-pass Homer had disastrous effects upon the one-time county seat.[29]

An intermediate goal of the HE&WT was Nacogdoches. This old Spanish town, which had been in existence for more than a hundred years, was the county seat of Nacogdoches County. It had a population in 1880 of 400 with nine general stores, a drug store, grocery, harness shop and a weekly newspaper, the *News.*[30] Although the town was situated on the old Spanish *El Camino Real,* the road had deteriorated into a series of holes, ruts, and ridges through which wagons and coaches lurched and groaned.

In wet weather the road was all but impassable and vehicles frequently bogged down. Travelers allowed two days for the thirty-five mile journey to San Augustine, camping out overnight. The town fathers had watched the progress of the "Bremond Road" northward with eagerness and some anxiety, certain that Nacogdoches was the natural intermediate terminal, fearful lest for some reason their town would be by-passed. The *News* regularly reported any new construction and chafed at the seemingly needless delays.[31]

After passing Lufkin, the road built rapidly to the Angelina River, which it crossed on a green-pine trestle to the bridgehead, purchased by Paul Bremond from the Vicente Michelli grant in 1879. Despite unusually heavy rains the crew built on to the station of Lewisville (often locally called Climax), about five miles from Nacogdoches, by the fall of 1882. There it halted to await the outcome of controversy and litigation concerning right-of-way. As late as February, 1883, the HE&WT advertised its trains only as far as Lewisville, which would connect with a "mail stage" for Nacogdoches. An advertisement in the *Houston Post* listed four trains daily: An express leaving Houston at 9:00 A.M. reached Lewisville at 6:30 P.M.; a local leaving Houston at 8:00 A.M. reached Lewisville at midnight. On the return trip the express left Lewisville at 9:30 A.M. and arrived in Houston at 6:45 P.M., while the local departed from Lewisville at 8:00 A.M. and reached the Houston terminal at 2 A.M. the following morning.[32]

Though the great majority of citizens eagerly awaited the coming of the railroad, a few opposed the request of the HE&WT for a right-of-way strip through their lands. One prominent Nacogdochean determined that this foreign monster was not going to cut down his fences, tear up his fields, divide his pasture lands, and frighten his cattle. Despite an adverse outcome of a court case in which the railroad exercised its right of eminent domain to cross these lands, this citizen armed himself with both a rifle and a shotgun, camped in the midst of his pasture, and dared the construction crew to touch his boundary fence. This stalemate ended only when some of the other leading citizens, who were concerned lest the threats and delay would cause Bremond to change the route, approached the irate landholder as friends, disarmed him, rolled him in a blanket, and carried him up the hill to the town. Meanwhile, the construction crew made haste to lay track through the disputed fields.[33]

The stipulations and restrictions which the landholders made in granting their land were many and varied. One owner deeded land for a right-of-way provided the road was built into the town before November 1, 1883. Another granted land for right-of-way and a depot but stipulated that the company could build one hotel and one saloon on the premises, and no more. Another stipulated that no saloons could be built on the property that he deeded. One landowner accepted for his land an "annual Pass so long as the railroad shall use the land." One Nacogdoches citizen required that in return for some 250 acres of land and some town lots that the railroad be promptly built into the town before November 1, 1883—that it locate its depot and warehouses on lots designated, and that "said railroad should run its train of cars thereto and blow its whistle thereat"—or the deed would be null and void.[34]

When the HE&WT finally made its way into Nacogdoches it was an occasion for civic celebrations, speeches, and banquets. The Houston press announced a new schedule to the railroad's new terminal: the express left Houston at 9:40 A.M. and arrived in Nacogdoches at 7:10 P.M. The return train left at 8:00 A.M. and reached Houston at 5:30 P.M. The local, or mixed train, left Houston at 7:10 A.M. and reached Nacogdoches at midnight. The return local left Nacogdoches at 6:00 A.M. and reached Houston at midnight. The distance from Houston was 140 miles.[35]

As might be expected, Nacogdoches experienced a boom. A year later the town was described by the editor of the local paper as "a city of 1,000 to 1,200 people—the present terminal of the HE&WT." It was said to be a town of thirty-five stores, five hotels, restaurants, and boarding houses, and several livery stables. The editor boasted that two magnificent brick business buildings had been erected during the past year and taxable property had increased some fifty percent in value. Plainly, the optimistic editor expected Nacogdoches, now that it had its railroad, to become the metropolis of the Piney Woods.[36]

HE&WT engine number 29
courtesy James T. Vogler, Harry J. Heaney, and Southern Pacific Company

III

Completion and Receivership

Before the end of 1883 construction on the HE&WT was underway again, and the narrow-gauge thrust its nose cautiously northward from Nacogdoches along Banita Creek. Turning northeast, the road built through a settled agricultural area and established the stations of Appleby, named for Bremond's son-in-law, James Appleby, who was auditor of the company, and Fitze in honor of General Freight and Passenger Agent Charles G. Fitze. The next year the HE&WT reached Garrison and by means of another green-pine trestle crossed the Attoyac River and passed out of Nacogdoches County.[1]

By the time the road reached Nacogdoches in 1883 the funds provided by the first mortgage bond issue were exhausted, and the directors and stockholders authorized Bremond to negotiate a new bond based on a second mortgage. The trustee was again the Union Trust Company of New York, and the amount of the bond was $750,000, at six percent interest and maturing in thirty years. Pledged as security for this loan was the road itself, beyond the claims of the holders of the first mortgage bonds, plus some 75,000 acres of timberland lying contiguous to the right-of-way in seven East Texas counties. Because of some irregularity in the ratification of these arrangements by the stockholders, it was necessary to re-submit the matter to the stockholders a second time, but after three meetings the second mortgage loan was duly approved by the directors and stockholders in the fall of 1884. By this time, the bonds had already been put on the market and partly sold.[2] This action provided funds needed to complete the road to the Louisiana line and bridge the Sabine River. It also raised the bonded indebtedness of the road to more than \$2,000,000, with fixed charges for interest alone of approximately \$140,000 per year.[3]

One source of income on which Bremond had counted to help finance the construction of his road was the state land grant. From 1852 until 1869, the State of Texas had granted public lands as a bounty for the building of railroads in the state, and the Constitution of 1876 directed the legislature to enact a general law continuing this encouragement. As a result, the state legislature in August 1876, passed an act giving sixteen sections of public land to each railroad company for every mile of road built after ten miles had been built, equipped, and put in running order. The company was required to lay at least a three-foot gauge and to survey one section of land for the state school fund for each section it received—the so called one-for-one survey. The railroad received the odd numbered sections, and the state retained the even numbered ones. The company was required to alienate one-half of its grant within six years and the rest within twelve years or else forfeit its claims.[4]

This law continued in effect for almost seven years, during which time the HE&WT built most of its track and received the appropriate number of land certificates. However, in the spring of 1882, the attention of the lawmakers was called to the simple statistical fact that already more acres of public land had been allotted to the several railroads than the state possessed. Consequently, the legislature promptly repealed the Railroad Land Grant Law on April 22, 1882. Only certificates that had already been issued were honored from that date, and as could be expected, there was great competition to find desirable land on which to file.[5]

The records of the General Land Office of Texas are somewhat confused, but it appears that only 1312 certificates for 839,680 acres representing eighty-two miles of completed track were actually issued to the HE&WT. Of these, only 1231 certificates were actually used to patent 787,840 acres of land. From the company records, it would appear that by the spring of 1882 the company had laid more than 120 miles of track and thus was entitled to 1920 certificates. Doubtless, Bremond, along with many other railroad builders, had not anticipated the sudden action of the legislature, and the act terminating the land grants caught him in the process of "proving up" some forty miles of road.[6]

The proceeds from the land certificates issued were disappointing. From the *Abstract of Texas Land Titles* it appears that the earliest HE&WT certificates were not filed until March, 1879, and the bulk of them were not filed until after 1880.[7] By this time most of the desirable lands in the public domain had been picked over and virtually all of the remaining lands lay west of the 100th meridian. The company exercised its option and located and surveyed 264 sections in the region northwest of San Antonio in Edwards, Crockett, Sutton, Real, and Kerr counties. The remaining certificates were sold to individuals, both settlers and speculators, who then used the certificates to acquire land wherever they could find it in the public domain. From the public records it is not clear whether these certificates were sold at one time in one huge lot or whether they were sold in smaller quantities over several years. Some private entries were dated as early as March, 1879, and large blocks of certificates were used to patent lands for individuals in June 1879. In all, HE&WT certificates were used to patent lands in more than sixty-five counties of the state. In addition to the five counties in which the company itself located land, most of the certificates were used to acquire lands in Presidio, Brewster, Schleicher, Tom Green, Webb, Bandera, Lynn, and Irion counties. The rest of the certificates were scattered over much of West Texas, from the Rio Grande Valley to the Panhandle.[8]

Bremond soon found, however, that it was necessary to sell off the lands already located in order to obtain funds for additional building. Accordingly, the directors authorized him to sell and convey 264 sections of land comprising 168,960 acres to J. M. Jamerson of New York for the sum of $40,000 in cash. This amounted to only twenty-four cents per acre. The company books are silent about the amounts received for the scrip.[9]

Bremond's efforts to place the HE&WT on a sound financial footing must have been indeed frustrating to the builder. The proposal to interest the businessmen of Houston in the venture was an obvious failure, although the road would, and did, channel into the city on the Buffalo Bayou most of the wealth of the Piney Woods.

Bremond originally planned to build the road directly northeast across Shelby County by way of Buena Vista to the Sabine River. In 1871 Buena Vista was described as a thriving village of more than twenty families and included a number of stores, a mill, and a blacksmith shop. At least one medical doctor and an attorney had their homes and offices there. The local tradition is, as was repeated in many similar cases, that the leading citizens of the village refused to donate land for right-of-way and buildings to the railroad and, indeed, demanded full market value for any land purchased. Bremond, who by this time was weary of the many delays encountered in building less than 250 miles of track, quickly had the right-of-way re-surveyed to cross the county in a gentle arc leaving the recalcitrant village two miles south of the road. As a result, other towns developed but Buena Vista disappeared.[10]

In the meantime, a sister railroad was chartered in Louisiana to build approximately forty miles of track from Shreveport to the state line on the Sabine River. Incorporated on June 9, 1883, the Gulf, Shreveport and Kansas City Railroad Company changed its name the next year to the Shreveport and Houston, and still later to the Houston and Shreveport. As the company was organized by largely the same people who controlled the HE&WT and as E. L. Bremond, son of the builder, served for a time as director and general manager, it too was known as "Bremond's Road." Beginning about May 1, 1884, the H&S built southward from Shreveport and reached Keachi the next year. After some delay while awaiting the arrival of additional rails and rolling stock, the road, under the direction of Superintendent J. R. Jones, resumed laying track and reached Logansport on the Sabine River by the fall of 1885. Like its Texas counterpart, the Houston and Shreveport was a single track, narrow-gauge road running through a heavily timbered pine forest on a lightly ballasted road bed and across streams and ravines on green-pine timber trestles. On reaching the Sabine, the H&S operated with a Y turnaround and carried local traffic while awaiting the coming of Bremond's Texas road and the junction.[11]

The HE&WT built slowly eastward to the state line, establishing three new towns en route. On a plateau east of the Attoyac Bayou, Paul Timpson, son of the company director Samuel C. Timpson, who had died in 1882, laid out a new town to be called Timpson. *The Nacogdoches News,* in July 1885, advertised a local train to Timpson every other day and noted that twenty cars of lumber had passed up to Timpson in a week in preparation for a big barbecue and lot sale to be held on Wednesday, August 1, 1885. Farther east, at a place destined later to be the junction point with the Santa Fe, the Hicks family established the town of Tenaha, named for an old Spanish municipality. Near the Sabine, the town of Joaquin was built by B. F. Morris, who donated 100 acres of land to the company on condition that the depot be located on his land. The town took its name from his child, Joaquin. By December 1, 1885, the HE&WT had reached the Sabine and completion of the project was within sight.[12]

But Paul Bremond did not live to see the fulfillment of his dream. On May 8, 1885, at the age of seventy-four and just ten years after the chartering of the HE&WT, Bremond died. A dispatch from Galveston in the late evening first carried the news. Under the heading "Another Gone" the account continued: "Colonel Paul Bremond, President of the Houston, East and West Texas narrow gauge Railway, died in this city tonight. His death occurred at the residence of Captain [E.] P. Lufkin, corner Avenue H and 25th Street at 7 P.M. and resulted from peritonitis. The deceased arrived in the city last Wednesday on a brief visit to his life-long friend Captain Lufkin. He had been in feeble health and hoped the change would prove beneficial. His death was sudden and somewhat unexpected although he was in his 75th year. His remains will be taken to Houston on the 9:30 train in the morning for interment."[13]

In Houston, the city editor of the *Post* commented on Bremond's passing as follows:

> As will be seen by the special dispatch from Galveston, Mr. Bremond died this evening at 7 P.M. Mr. Bremond was one of the most remarkable men in the South. He came to Texas while quite young and located at Houston, where for many years he carried on successful mercantile pursuits. He conceived the project of building a railroad from the Gulf to the Red River which resulted in the orga-

> nization and construction of that splendid line of railways piercing the heart of Texas known as the Houston and Texas Central Railway. Toward the construction of the mainline of this system Mr. Bremond contributed largely from his own private means. He became the 1st president of the road and maintained an active interest in it for many years. Several years ago he projected the Houston, East and West Texas narrow gauge railway running from Houston to Shreveport when completed. At the time of his death he had finished and was operating 200 miles of railway, every foot of which was built from Mr. Bremond's own fortune, without recourse to the usual methods of selling watered stock and issuing blanket mortgages. The balance of the road, some 135 miles, was under contract for immediate construction at the time of his death. The deceased was known throughout Texas as "the father of Railroads." His loss will be severely felt. He leaves a widow and an interesting family of six grown children. Deceased was married three times. His fortune is variously estimated at between 2 and 3 millions [sic]. Mr. Bremond was a firm believer in the modern doctrine of spiritualism.[14]

Three days later, after the funeral, the editor of the *Post* paid his last respects to the "Builder." He wrote as follows:

> When the clods fell on the coffin of Paul Bremond last Sunday, the last honors were paid to the remains of a good citizen and a remarkable man. The man who makes two blades of grass grow where

but one existed has been pronounced a benefactor to the human race; Bremond made harvests wave where nothing prevailed but the spontaneous productions of nature. Men are praised who by skillful combination of resources, have introduced what may be termed the syndicate era in business affairs and have thus realized important results. Bremond, single-handed and alone, fought out his enterprises and died, unhappily, just as the consummation of his great work would have gladdened his heart and crowned his self-sacrificing labors with success. The annals of Texas are ornamented by names that illustrate manly energy, prudence and steady will; but they present none that suggest superiority to the name of Paul Bremond in these respects. In spite of difficulties, impediments and disasters that would have disgusted and appalled a man of lighter caliber and less nerve, Mr. Bremond pushed on his work in building the Houston, East & West Texas Railway with a determination and vigor, which won him the respect of men of his grade and the lasting gratitude of the people. The newspapers have been full of eulogistic mention of his private virtues and his successful achievement as a capitalist and Railroad builder, and the *Post* is unwilling to suffer the grass to grow on the grave of so honored and useful citizen without adding revernetually [sic] its chaplet of memorial flowers. It has already expressed in its local columns the grief expressed by the Houston public at their loss and the estimation in which the deceased was held, and now it would add—when the mournful scene has closed and the earth has received back into its bosom the

> form that was the earthly abode of Paul Bremond's spirit—the deliberate words of respect and affection for one who was a practical benefactor to his people and who sleeps well after his heavy and exhausting work was done.[15]

In an editorial on his passing, the *San Antonio Express* called him a peculiar man with many idiosyncrasies but said that these were anything but vagaries when results were calculated. The editor conceded that Bremond was not a popular man and had made many bitter enemies, but he contended that he had left two monuments, the H&TC and HE&WT railroads, which would not have been built had it not been for him. For all his peculiarities, concluded the editor, he was an upbuilder and a benefactor of mankind.[16] Certainly the East Texas region would have had to wait many more years for a rail outlet if Paul Bremond had not determined to build a road through the Piney Woods.

In retrospect, it is apparent that Paul Bremond was unlike the stereotype of the railroad tycoon which has been preserved in many texts and popular writings. Far from getting rich, Bremond lost heavily in both of his railroad ventures. Evidently he was successful in general merchandising and entrepreneurial ventures in Houston and Galveston. In these he acquired a reputation as a person of property and enterprise. But his earlier rail building effort had ended in receivership, and he lost control of the H&TC despite its many advantages and favorable route. The HE&WT was destined for the same fate.

It was unfortunate that Bremond became enamoured with the narrow-gauge railroad, for by 1876 the "standard gauge" had already become prevalent and most odd gauges, both wide and narrow, were converting to the 4 feet, 8-1/2 inch gauge. By the time the HE&WT was completed in 1886, other southern roads had voted to adopt standard gauge, and narrow gauge main line railroads were rapidly disappearing. Full interchange of traffic at Houston and Shreveport would have been much more feasible if the HE&WT had been standard gauge. Yet apparently Bremond never recanted from his narrow gauge heresy.

It is even questionable if Bremond's grand scheme to build a railroad through the Piney Woods just at this time was wisely conceived. From the first, the project was inadequately financed. Reserve funds were lacking and the project failed to attract appreciable support from the business leaders of Houston. And Bremond's subsequent efforts to secure funds from the interior towns and villages were at best a forlorn hope. It should not have taken a financial wizard to determine that these isolated, mud-caked East Texas towns had no investment capital available for any enterprise, including the building of a railroad. Essentially the HE&WT was built with Bremond's personal funds, his personal credit, and the mortgage loans from the Union Trust Company of New York. His heirs lost heavily in the debacle that followed his death.

Thus, it can safely be concluded that the persistent promotion of the HE&WT by Paul Bremond was impelled by a vision of need and public service rather than any profit-making motive. Like other railway dreamers, he was obsessed with the desire to open up the Piney Woods and bring progress and civilization to the East Texas region. This would at the same time provide a direct route to the populous areas of the Northeast and help consolidate Houston as the rail center of the Southwest. As such, Paul Bremond well deserves the title of "Builder" and should be rescued from the oblivion into which he has fallen. Then, it may be hoped, that the spirit of Moseley Baker will again rest in peace.

It was a sad and dispirited group of directors that met on June 26, 1885, "to choose a director to replace Paul Bremond, late president who has died." Mrs. Mary Louise Bremond, principal stockholder and executrix of her husband's estate, indicated that she wished E. P. Hill of Houston to represent her interests and he was duly elected director. Another director had resigned, and Edward L. Bremond, son of the builder, was elected to replace him. A week later, the directors voted that the "present financial status of the company made it imperative that the road be placed in the hands of a receivership" and M. G. Howe of Houston was appointed on July 8, 1885, to act as receiver by the court. At the December stockholders' meeting Mrs. Bremond was present, and with E. P. Hill serving as chairman of the meeting a new group of directors was chosen: T. W. House, W. E. Lufkin, James Appleby, and William Marsh Rice. To those who were not previously stockholders Mrs. Bremond transferred one share of stock each.[17] New officers included T. W. House, president; E. P. Hill, vice-president; E. Dargan, secretary; with House doubling as treasurer. W. E. Lufkin proposed and it was agreed that the officers would serve without compensation in view of the company's shaky financial condition.

In the meantime, the construction crews rapidly closed the gap to the Louisiana line. By December 1885, both the HE&WT and the H&S had reached the banks of the Sabine and were awaiting the completion of the bridge across the river. This structure, built by the King Iron Bridge and Manufacturing Company, had been under construction since the previous year. All materials for it prior to the completion of the rail lines were brought up the Sabine by steamboat or hauled overland by mule and oxen from Shreveport. Company officials and the interested public on both sides of the Sabine waited impatiently for the completion of this final link between the Gulf coast and Shreveport, the gateway to the East. The *Houston Post* reported on January 26, 1886, that "word arrived here that late last evening a work train passed over the Sabine River from Texas to Louisiana on the new false works, making contact between Houston and Shreveport, Louisiana, via the HE&WT narrow gauge and the Shreveport and Houston narrow gauge railway. The new iron bridge will now be completed. This connection will give this city an eastern outlet via Logansport." The next day the *Dallas Morning News* announced that the "H&S, generally known as Bremond's narrow-gauge, was completed at six o'clock this evening as far as track laying is concerned. The new road is 232 miles long, and gives Texas a new outlet to the Eastern cities independent of the Texas pool. . . ." In Houston, General Agent R. S. Collins of the HE&WT wrote on January 27 that "we have driven the last spike and hope to have our regular trains running through to Shreveport in a few days." Both passenger and freight service began immediately. *The Nacogdoches News* issue of January 30, 1886, announced the "first through train from Houston to Shreveport left Houston at 7:15 this morning and passed this point at 4 P.M. The *News* of today will be read in Shreveport at 9:45 tonight."[18] The road was completed. Paul Bremond's narrow-gauge had opened up the Piney Woods to the outside world.

IV

Financial Structure, Organization and Operations

From the very inception of the HE&WT its owners depended heavily upon lumber traffic, and to a lesser extent upon cotton, for its principal revenue. Indeed, the HE&WT cut through a magnificent stand of twelve million acres of virgin long-leaf and short-leaf pine timber which could not be exploited well until the arrival of rail transportation. Prior to the penetration of the Piney Woods by the railroads, other states, particularly Florida, supplied most of the timber for Texas homes, and the long hauls by ship or rail greatly increased the cost of lumber at the building site. With the coming of the railroads into East Texas the lumber business boomed, and the annual cut increased spectacularly from less than 100,000,000 board feet in 1869 to 300,000,000 in 1879; 770,000,000 in 1889; and 1,200,000,000 in 1900.[1] A fair share of this growing traffic would have enabled the HE&WT to meet the payments on its bonds and earn a profit. Unfortunately, the first owners were not able to wait for the development of this lumber traffic. Although the HE&WT was favorably placed with its line running directly through the center of the Piney Woods and without any direct parallel line competition, the lumber tonnage would have to be developed promptly for Bremond's road to survive.

The Houston press maintained a keen interest both in the construction of track and the development of lumber traffic. In a story in the spring of 1878 the *Telegraph* related the details of an inspection trip by state officials to certify the eligibility of the road for the state land grant. The reporter commented, with obvious satisfaction, that five sawmills were seen along the forty-mile route, with a combined capacity of 100,000 board feet per day.[2] Two years later the *Post* reported that "HE&WT is bringing in big trains of lumber" every week. A week later the same paper stated mournfully that because of the strike of Houston dock and terminal hands the "narrow gauge" had brought in only a little lumber that week. It did not run empty, however, for the passenger train brought 125 passengers for the circus which was playing at Houston.[3]

Builder Paul Bremond was optimistic about the prospects of his railroad. In the late fall of 1880 he reported that the HE&WT was being run with an operating expense of less than thirty percent of its gross earnings. He speculated that its earnings would be even better if the Houston broad-gauge roads were not so overburdened that they could transfer promptly and give the HE&WT freer use of its rolling stock. During October alone the "narrow gauge" brought into Houston 376 cars of lumber and could have brought more but for the inability of the local lines to transfer. To maintain this volume of traffic new mills were needed as the road proceeded north, and Bremond lost no opportunity to organize inspection tours for prospective business men and regularly stressed the advantages of locating a mill or processing plant along the route. For example, the town of Burke, established in 1881, only four years later had three sawmills and three cotton gins to add to the traffic of the HE&WT.[4]

Fares and freight earnings, however, were extremely modest in the early years. For example, during the first quarter of 1878 the earnings did not reach $500 for any month.[5] Later in the year lumber shipments began to materialize and the earnings improved. In August 1878, earnings totaled $4,523.58 (including $3,280.91 for hauling lumber), September: $3,287.41, and October: $4,240.18. A year later the freight earnings for December 1879, were listed as $8,395.87.[6] By this date the first mortgage bonds had been authorized, issued, and partly sold, amounting to some $1,344,000 at seven percent with interest charges of $94,000 per annum. Even at the favorable level of December 1879, the total earnings would barely pay the interest on the bonded debt, to say nothing of operating expenses, maintenance, or dividends to the stockholders.

By 1882 the HE&WT had reached Nacogdoches County and most of the funds from the first mortgage bonds had been spent for construction, rolling stock, and equipment. Freight earnings had climbed to $305,396.06 (less $23,068.46 for direct charges), and passenger fares grossed $38,481.79 for a total of $320,739.61.[7] In addition there were sales of Lufkin town lots, sale of surplus property, U.S. mail and telegraph contracts, and news butcher receipts. Payrolls for the same year totaled $151,612.23, or a monthly average of $13,000. A consolidated statement of expenses, less payrolls, for this period averaged $7,000 per month, or $85,000 annually. Thus, even with this improved earnings picture the road was forced to rely on minor and miscellaneous income to meet its fixed payments.[8] Clearly, more than the local traffic of the Piney Woods was essential if "Bremond's Road" were to survive.

As of 1883 *Poor's Manual of Railroads* listed the HE&WT as having ten locomotives, eight passenger cars, four baggage cars, 546 freight cars, and twelve handcars. Its length was 140 miles, its northern terminal Nacogdoches, and its gauge three feet. In a summary statement for the year it listed $307,875 gross earnings and $199,992 in net earnings. Construction costs were

$137,061 and interest on bonds was $56,795, leaving a favorable balance of $6,135. By 1885 the total length had grown to 192 miles and its rolling stock had increased to sixteen locomotives, eight passenger cars, five combination cars, four baggage cars, and 617 freight cars. It listed the capital stock at $1,920,000, bonded indebtedness at $1,344,000 first mortgage, and $750,000 second mortgage. The floating debt was $160,172. Assets included the value of railroad, rolling stock, and equipment at $3,448,125; 75,000 acres of land valued at $5.00 per acre at $375,000; and properties and town lots at $100,000. By its own summary the liabilities of "Bremond's Road" exceeded its assets by more than $250,000. *Poor's* listing for 1887 showed the road under receivership with the note that it had defaulted on its first mortgage bonds as of November 1, 1886. The rolling stock was the same as the 1885 listing, indicating that since the death of the builder only the minimum had been spent on maintenance and nothing on improving the road. The same summary noted that the Houston and Shreveport Railway had been organized in 1884 by parties affiliated with the HE&WT and the connection between the roads had been completed on January 26, 1886. The H&S had also been placed in the hands of receivers on July 8, 1885, but was restored to the company December 1, 1885, and continued to operate under its own managers until 1889.[9]

In 1886, the first year the road was completed to Shreveport as well as the first year of receivership, the records show a continued loss. Freight gross earnings amounted to $320,000 and passenger earnings to $44,000 that year, but expenses were also up. Construction for that year totaled $53,000, and receiver's certificates took $102,000. The interest on the bonded debt amounted to $94,140. The balance sheet showed a net loss of $133,218.49.[10]

In an analysis of nearly fifty railroads in the South at this same period, railroad historian John F. Stover found that the roads forced into receivership were characterized by an unfavorable ratio of bonded debt to stock issue, excessive capitalization per mile of road, and weak earnings equaling only some five to ten percent of their funded debt.[11] By comparison, the HE&WT, based on *Poor's* data for 1887, had a bond-stock ratio of fifty-two to forty-eight. The lightly ballasted three-foot-gauge road was capitalized at $21,740 per mile, and its earnings equaled only eight percent of its funded debt. This summary, unfavorable as it was, actually would have been even more unfavorable when it is remembered that little of the capital stock outstanding represented cash paid into the company. Instead, a considerable amount of stock was distributed to Bremond and other directors for "services rendered." It is doubtful if much over $1,000,000 was actually paid in for stock purchases.

The HE&WT was unable to rally from its heavy bonded debt and weak earnings. Though it continued to operate for seven years under the receivership of M. G. Howe, it was finally sold at auction from the courthouse step in Houston as a result of foreclosure action brought by several private bondholders. At the foreclosure sale, August 2, 1892, the road and all its assets were purchased by Elbert S. Jemison acting for the Union Trust Company for $1,200,000. There seem to have been no other serious bidders. The Houston and Shreveport Railroad, likewise in receivership under M. G. Howe after 1889, was sold to Joseph Richardson and Marcus C. Hawley of New York on July 15, 1891. Under their new owners and assigns both roads were completely reorganized.[12]

Prior to his death Paul Bremond, as president and chairman of the board of directors, ran the HE&WT as a feudal barony, which perhaps it was. Friend and business associate Abraham Groesbeck served as vice-president, son-in-law Samuel C. Timpson acted as secretary, and another son-in-law, J. A. Dozier, served as treasurer. Later, yet another son-in-law, James Appleby, was the auditor. Bremond's son by his first marriage, E. L. Bremond, served the family interests as president of the allied Houston and Shreveport Railroad at the same time that he was general manager of the HE&WT. In addition to their usual duties all members of the managerial group engaged in promotional activities under Bremond's direction. Below the top echelon D. D. Figuet and Charles G. Fitze successively served as general freight and passenger agent and tried, unsuccessfully, to cope with the critical problem of weak earnings and high fixed costs. A number of men, including E. P. Lufkin and G. G. Woodbridge, held the title of chief engineer and were responsible for construction and maintenance of the line. All of these specialists operated under the instructions or even the whims of the president.

After Bremond's death, T. W. House held the dual positions of president and treasurer but served under the supervision of M. G. Howe, the court-appointed receiver, from July 1885, until 1892. E. P. Hill, who represented Mrs. Bremond's interests, was vice-president for a time during the same period, as was J. F. Crosby. During much of the receivership Eugene Dargan was secretary and auditor. The younger Bremond relinquished his position as general manager of the HE&WT but continued as president of the H&S until 1890. The records of the company disclose the names of R. S. Collins, C. D. Stinson, William Doherty, R. D. Yoakum, Horace Cone, W. H. Darney, and T. J. Anderson, who served either as general passenger and freight agent or general passenger agent during the period of the receivership.

Along the route of the HE&WT the station agent served as the local representative of the railroad and was a person of considerable importance in his community. The records of their remittances preserved in the surviving company ledgers indicate that local business originating from the interior towns was small and prior to 1892 rather irregular. The list of station agents' names between 1881 and 1899 disclosed that the positions were relatively stable as many agents served a town for a number of years. Also it is apparent that the HE&WT moved its employees up and down the line, evidently rewarding good work with a better job. The list, not necessarily in order of service, is as follows:[13]

Houston	W. F. Simmons, M. Everett, A. C. Alexander, S. P. Coughlin, A. M. Gentry, W. T. Purviance, P. Briscoe
Cleveland	W. P. Johnson, T. M. Peebles
Shepherd	G. M. Bynum, T. S. Sears, W. C. Roberts, J. F. O'Connor
Goodrich	H. A. Magill, P. M. Perkins, W. A. Woody, E. A. Bryan
Livingston	J. T. Estill, B. F. Haynes, J. E. Burton
Moscow	B. F. Haynes, C. M. Adams, P. M. Perkins
Corrigan	C. P. Humphrey, G. W. Pence, W. A. Woody
Burke	L. B. Bright, D. B. McCall
Lufkin	A. R. Moore, W. S. Carter, F. C. Sears, G. T. Porter
Lewisville	
Nacogdoches	L. F. D. Lesdenier, C. D. Stinson
Appleby	J. A. Looney, A. B. Stoddard
Garrison	A. W. Cheeseman, J. L. Faubian
Timpson	John Collins, H. R. Forey
Teneha	A. J. Clayton, J. A. Looney
Joaquin	Mrs. C. D. Wofford, Mrs. C. W. Taylor
Logansport	R. J. Alexander, W. C. Roberts, B. F. Haynes
Franks	J. W. Williams
Keachi	W. I. F. Russell
Keithville	Keith Brothers
Shreveport	L. P. Davidson, P. A. Lacy, F. M. Donohue, B. F. Haynes, A. W. C. Cheeseman.

One of the most interesting phases of the operation of a railroad is the development of its schedules. A typical listing of the stations and stops on the HE&WT and H&S included the following running from southwest to northeast: Houston, Seasonburg,

San Jacinto, Parker, Hacknew, Merriman, New Caney, Cleveland, Africa, Round Prairie, Shepherd, Trinity River, Goodrich, Livingston, Leggett, Moscow, Natchez City, Burke, Lufkin, Lewisville, Nacogdoches, Appleby, Fitze, Garrison, Blair, Timpson, Bobo, Teneha, Paxton, Joaquin, Logansport, Franks, Keachi, Keithville, and Shreveport. The progress of "Bremond's Road" can be seen by comparing its passenger schedules as it built slowly northward.

The earliest schedule available for the HE&WT was for the weekly Sunday excursion to San Jacinto Springs, announced in the spring of 1878:

Houston, East and West Texas Railway
Excursion to San Jacinto Springs
Sunday, April 21, 1878.

Trains will leave Houston:	Arrive at Springs:
9 A.M.	10 A.M.
2:30 P.M.	3:30 P.M.
4:15 P.M.	5:15 P.M.

Round trip—50 cents—children, 25 cents.—Fishing, swimming, picnicking, dancing. Strict order maintained. No spirits.
Added attraction: Band Concert, St. Louis Band.

(signed) Paul Bremond, Pres.
HE&WT Ry.

Though it rained on the evening of April 21 and thus partly spoiled the excursion, other Sunday excursions were advertised with essentially the same schedule and attractions throughout the summer of 1878.[14]

The earliest regularly scheduled passenger service was advertised in the Houston press in May of the same year.[15]

Houston, East and West Texas Railroad
Daily Train Service to Caney

Leaves Houston:	9:00 A.M.
Arrives back in Houston:	5:00 P.M.

Before the end of 1878 the line was extended to Cleveland and the schedule changed to read:[16]

Houston, East and West Texas Railway
Daily Train Service to Caney and Cleveland

Leave Houston:	9:00 A.M.
Arrives back in Houston:	5:00 P.M.

By February 1883, the company announced that the road had now reached the outskirts of Nacogdoches (as indeed it had since November 1882) a distance of 135 miles:[17]

Houston, East and West Texas Railway
Trains now run to Lewisville
Four trains daily

Leaves Houston:	Arrives Lewisville:
9:00 A.M.	6:30 P.M. (express)
8:00 A.M.	12:00 P.M. (local)
Leaves Lewisville:	Arrives Houston:
9:30 A.M.	6:45 P.M.(express)
8:00 A.M.	2:00 A.M. [sic] (local)

All trains will connect with mail stage for
Nacogdoches—five miles distant.

When the road finally reached Nacogdoches and a depot was built, more elaborate advertisements read as follows:[18]

Houston, East & West Texas Railway
Shortest Route Through East Texas
Daily Trains from
Houston to Nacogdoches
140 miles
Elegant Passenger Coaches
Polite and Accommodating Conductors

Trains leave Houston:		Trains Arrive Houston:	
Express 9:00 A.M.		Express	5:20 P.M.
Mixed	8:20 A.M.	Mixed	1:00 A.M.
Freight*	7:30 A.M.	Freight	7:15 P.M.
(leave) Nacogdoches:		(arrive) Nacogdoches:	
Express 8:00 A.M.		Express	6:30 P.M.
Mixed	8:05 A.M.	Mixed	1:40 A.M.
Corrigan:		Corrigan:	
Freight Daily	9:00 A.M.	Freight Daily	1:40 P.M.

*For further information as to Freights
and passage address Houston, Texas

E. L. Bremond,	Chas. G. Fitze,
Gen. Mgr.	Gen Freight and
	Passenger Agent.

After the completion of the road and the opening of the bridge across the Sabine the company offered a revised schedule as follows:[19]

Houston, East & West Texas Railway
Shortest Route Throughout East Texas
Daily Trains from
Houston to Nacogdoches
140 miles
Elegant Passenger Coaches
Polite and Accommodating Conductors

Trains Leave:		Trains Arrive:	
Houston:		Houston:	
Express	7:15 A.M.	Express	9:45 P.M.
Freight	7:30 A.M.	Freight	8:00 A.M.
Shreveport:		Shreveport:	
Express	7:15 A.M.	Express	9:45 P.M.
Freight	8:00 A.M.	Freight	8:00 A.M.

Pass Nacogdoches

West Bound	1:07 P.M.	East Bound	3:00 P.M.

For further information as to freights and passage, address

M.G. Howe, Receiver — R. S. Collins, Gen. F. & P .A.

A still later notice featured connection points: [20]

Houston, East and West Texas Railway

Shortest route through East Texas, making close connections at Houston with the H&TC, So. Pac., and GC&SF Rys., for all points in Northwest and South Texas without layover. Also connects with SA&AP & I&GN Railroads.

Trains leave Houston:	8:30 A.M.
Shreveport:	6:00 A.M.
Trains pass Nacogdoches:	
East Bound	4:47 P.M.
West Bound	11:10 A.M.
Trains Arrive:	
Shreveport	10:00 P.M.
Houston	8:00 P.M.

Connects at Shreveport with the Queen and Crescent for all points East and North, and the Texas and Pacific Ry. for all points in West Texas.

M.G. Howe, Receiver — C. D. Stinson, Nacogdoches Agt.

R. S. Collins, G. P. Agent.

About the same time another advertisement read as follows:[21]

Houston, East & West Texas

and

Shreveport and Houston

Railways

Connects at Shreveport with Queen & Crescent, Texas & Pacific and St. Louis, Arkansas and Texas R.R. All trains connect at Lufkin with the St.LA&T Ry. At Houston with all roads diverging. Corrigan with T&S Rd.

—No. 1—

Leaves Houston	8:30 A.M.
Leaves Lufkin	3:40 P.M.
Arrives Nacogdoches	4:47 P.M.
Arrives Garrison	5:55 P.M.
Arrives Shreveport	10:00 P.M.

—No. 2—

Leaves Shreveport	6:00 A.M.
Arrives Garrison	9:59 A.M.
Arrives Nacogdoches	11:10 A.M.
Arrives Houston	8:00 P.M.

For further information address

	R.S. Collins.
M.G. Howe,	General Passenger Agent
Rec. HE&WT and S&H Ry.	
	Houston, Texas.

Some of the advertisements at the turn of the century were even more elaborate and separated the general card from the local schedule. A typical notice appeared in the *Nacogdoches Sentinel*:[22]

Houston, East and West Texas Railway
Houston and Shreveport Railway
"Through the Heart of the Lumber, Fruit and
Oil Regions of Texas."
Through trains with
Pullman Standard
Sleeping Cars.
Between
Houston and Shreveport, La.
Special rates to Summer Resorts in
Texas and Points Northeast and West.

T. J. Anderson, G. P. Agent.

Special excursion rates to Houston were featured in this advertisement in 1889:[23]

HOUSTON, EAST & WEST TEXAS RAILWAY
&
SHREVEPORT AND HOUSTON RY.

Gives all an opportunity to witness the grand display of Military (Houston) at the following reduced fares for Round Trip.

Cleveland	$2.80	Nacogdoches	$5.65
Shepherd	3.05	Garrison	6.00
Livingston	3.65	Timpson	6.00
Moscow	4.10	Tenaha	6.00
Corrigan	4.30	Logansport	6.00
Burke	4.85	Keachi	6.65
Lufkin	5.05	Shreveport	7.60

Tickets will be on sale
from June 1 to June 14th.
Good till June 18th.

M. G. Howe, Receiver

R . S. Collins, G.P.A.

Shay hauling logs
courtesy East Texas Research Center

Loading logs with mules
courtesy East Texas Research Center

Houston East & West Texas R'y, Houston & Shreveport R. R.

LOCAL TIME TABLES.

BETWEEN HOUSTON AND LOGANSPORT AND SHREVEPORT.

EAST-BOUND. No. 3. Mixed. Daily.	No. 1. Shreveport and Kansas City Mail and Express Daily.	Dist. from Houston.		STATIONS. February 19th, 1899.		Dist. from Shreveport.	WEST-BOUND. No. 2. Houston and Galveston Mail and Express Daily.	No. 4. Mixed. Daily.
	7 00PM		Lv	GALVESTON (G.LaP.&H.R'y)	Ar.		9 50AM	
	8 50PM		Ar	HOUSTON (H.&T.C.Depot)	Ar.		8 00AM	
7 30AM	9 05PM	.0	Lv	Houston	Ar.N	232.0	6 40AM	7 30PM
	9 10PM		Lv	I. & G. N. Crossing	Ar.		6 37AM	6 34PM
8 36AM	9 32PM	9.0	Lv	Lock	Ar.	223.0	f 6 06AM	6 04PM
9 05AM	9 52PM	17.0	Lv	Humble	Ar.D	215.0	5 50AM	5 19PM
9 30AM	10 10PM	23.2	Lv	Japan	Ar.	208.8	5 32AM	4 49PM
10 00AM	10 25PM	28.3	Lv	New Caney	Ar.D	203.7	5 17AM	4 04PM
10 32AM	10 45PM	36.5	Lv	Midline	Ar.	195.5	f 4 56AM	3 34PM
11 50AM	11 02PM	43.1	Lv	Cleveland	Ar.N	188.9	4 39AM	2 59PM
12 15PM	11 15PM	48.5	Lv	Smiths	Ar.	183.5	f 4 25AM	2 19PM
1 15PM	11 32PM	55.2	Lv	Shepherd	Ar.D	176.8	4 08AM	1 49PM
1 49PM	11 44PM	60.0	Lv	Urbana	Ar.	172.0	f 3 55AM	1 29PM
2 09PM	f11 52PM	63.4	Lv	Goodrich	Ar.D	168.6	3 46AM	1 09PM
2 29PM	12 01AM	67.2	Lv	Baldwin	Ar.	164.8	3 37AM	12 49PM
3 02PM	12 12AM	71.4	Lv	Livingston	Ar.N	160.6	3 26AM	11 39AM
3 54PM	12 35AM	79.6	Lv	Leggett	Ar.D	152.4	3 02AM	11 03AM
4 22PM	12 47AM	83.8	Lv	Vaida	Ar.	148.2	2 51AM	10 30AM
5 00PM	12 57AM	87.5	Lv	Moscow	Ar.D	144.5	2 41AM	9 50AM
5 50PM	1 13AM	92.9	Ar	Corrigan	Lv.N	139.1	2 27AM	9 50AM
5 50PM	1 13AM	92.9	Lv	Corrigan	Ar.N	139.1	2 27AM	8 50AM
6 20PM	1 31AM	98.7	Lv	Fants	Ar.	133.3	f 2 11AM	8 25AM
6 40PM	1 43AM	103.0	Lv	Renova	Ar.	129.0	1 59AM	8 10AM
6 55PM f	1 51AM	106.0	Lv	Emporia	Ar.D	126.0	f 1 51AM	7 15AM
7 50PM	2 03AM	110.2	Lv	Burke	Ar.D	121.8	1 33AM	6 30AM
8 30PM	2 23AM	118.1	Ar	Lufkin	Lv.N	113.9	1 12AM	6 30AM
7 00AM	2 28AM	118.1	Lv	Lufkin	Ar.N	113.9	1 07AM	8 30PM
8 00AM f	2 58AM	129.6	Lv	Lanana	Ar.	102.4	f12 36AM	6 30PM
9 20AM	3 19AM	138.0	Ar	Nacogdoches	Lv.N	94.0	12 14AM	5 45PM
9 20AM	3 19AM	138.0	Lv	Nacogdoches	Ar.N	94.0	12 14AM	5 45PM
9 48AM	3 34AM	143.7	Lv	Redfield	Ar.	88.3	11 58PM	4 50PM
10 08AM	3 44AM	147.4	Lv	Appleby	Ar.D	84.6	11 49PM	4 31PM
10 23AM	3 51AM	149.9	Lv	Sterne	Ar.	82.1	f11 42PM	4 17PM
10 48AM	4 03AM	154.3	Lv	Fitze	Ar.	77.7	11 31PM	3 50PM
11 30AM	4 14AM	158.3	Lv	Garrison	Ar.D	73.7	11 20PM	3 25PM
11 50AM	4 24AM	162.2	Lv	Blair	Ar.		11 08PM	3 02PM
12 30PM	4 35AM	166.7	Lv	Timpson	Ar.N	65.3	10 56PM	2 40PM
12 55PM f	4 47AM	171.6	Lv	Bobo	Ar.	60.4	f10 42PM	2 05PM
1 35PM	4 59AM	176.3	Lv	Tenaha	Ar.D	55.7	10 29PM	1 35PM
2 35PM	5 29AM	188.0	Lv	Joaquin	Ar.D	44.0	9 57PM	12 20PM
2 55PM	5 38AM	192.0	Ar	LOGANSPORT	Lv.D	40.0	9 46PM	12 05PM
3 10PM	5 38AM	192.0	Lv	LOGANSPORT	Ar.D	40.0	9 46PM	11 50AM
4 00PM f	6 00AM	201.5	Lv	Franks	Ar.	30.5	f 9 21PM	11 00AM
4 35PM	6 16AM	208.2	Lv	Keachie	Ar.D	23.8	9 04PM	10 25AM
5 02PM f	6 28AM		Lv	Preston	Ar.		f 8 50PM	9 58AM
5 35PM	6 43AM	219.6	Lv	Keithville	Ar.	12.4	8 34PM	9 25AM
6 10PM	6 55AM	224.7	Lv	Larosen	Ar.	7.3	f 8 19PM	9 00AM
			Lv	Shreveport Junction	Ar.			
7 00PM	7 12AM	232.0	Lv	Shreveport (H. & S. Depot)	Ar.D	.0	8 00PM	8 30AM
	7 20AM		Ar	SHREVEPORT (K. C. P. & G. Depot)	Lv.		7 50PM	

Through Sleeping Cars between Houston, Galveston and Kansas City.

f Stop only on signal.

Passengers should always purchase tickets at stations where they are sold, to avoid extra charge made on trains.

2

HE&WT time table, 1899

MECHANICAL DEPARTMENT

Houston East & West Texas R'y.

RECORD OF EQUIPMENT.

8 Wheeled Passenger Locomotives.
Built 1893 - Brooks Locomotive Works.
Diameter and Stroke of Cylinder 17" x 24".
Diameter of Driving Wheels - 72".
Driving Wheel Base, 9 ft.
Engine Wheel Base, 23 ft. 9 in.
Total Wheel Base, Engine and Tender, 45 ft. 8 in.
Diameter Boiler 52 in. - 202 Tubes, 2 In.
Length and Width of Fire Box, 34" x 78".
Weight, On Drivers 65,100 lbs. - On Truck 39,500 lbs.
Total Weight of Engine, in Working Order, 104,600 lbs.
Weight of Tank - loaded - 89,500 lbs. - Capacity, 3,100 gals
Steam Pressure, 170 lbs.
Steel Tired Engine Truck and Tender Wheels.
Westinghouse ~~Push Down Cam~~ Driver Brakes.
Automatic Couplers - front and rear.
Purchased from L. S. & M. S. R. R., March 1900.
Number Owned - 2.

HE&WT passenger locomotive number 8
courtesy Southern Pacific Company

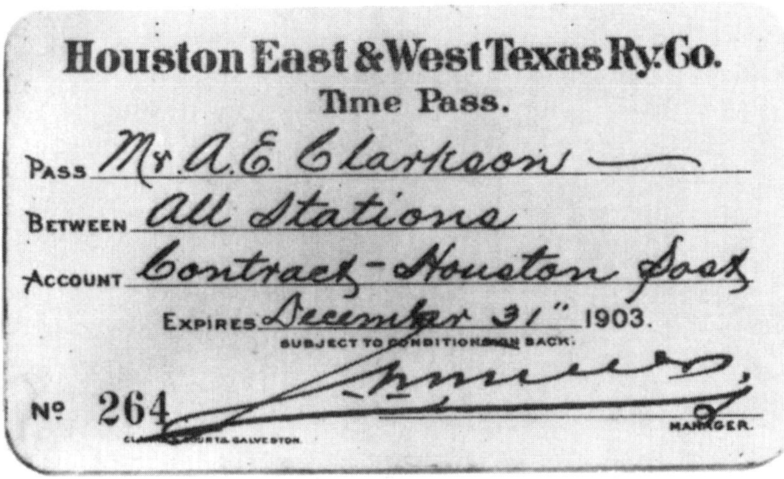
Houston East & West Texas Ry. Co.
Time Pass.
Pass Mr A.E. Clarkson
Between All Stations
Account Contract - Houston Post
Expires December 31" 1903.
SUBJECT TO CONDITIONS ON BACK.
No 264
Manager.

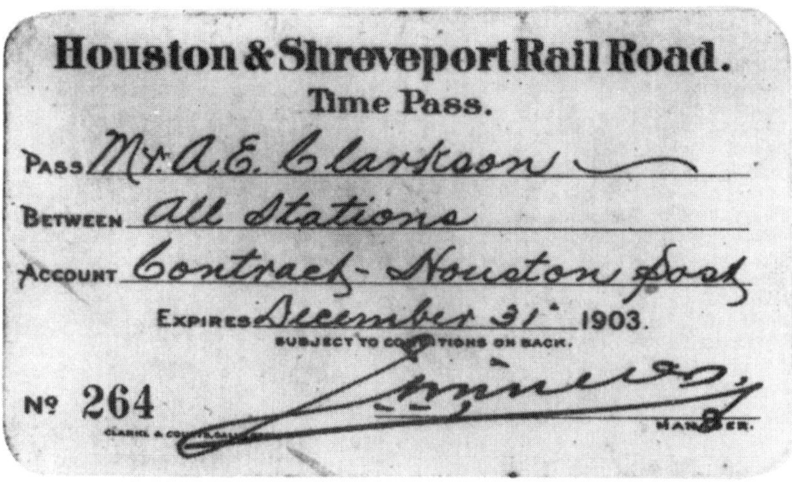
Houston & Shreveport Rail Road.
Time Pass.
Pass Mr A.E. Clarkson
Between All Stations
Account Contract - Houston Post
Expires December 31" 1903.
SUBJECT TO CONDITIONS ON BACK.
No 264
Manager.

courtesy Harry J. Heaney

Laying rails through the Piney Woods
courtesy East Texas Research Center

Steel gang laying rails
courtesy East Texas Research Center

Unloading logs at mill
courtesy East Texas Research Center

Thompson Brothers engine
courtesy East Texas Research Center

Logging crew
courtesy East Texas Research Center

Shay locomotive
courtesy East Texas Research Center

Logging the Piney Woods
courtesy East Texas Research Center

V

Reorganization and Consolidation

Following the foreclosure sale on August 2, 1892, the HE&WT was completely reorganized. A new company, but with the same name, came into being, and the property was delivered to it and the receivership terminated. In the new organization, Elbert S. Jemison was president, T. W. House was secretary, and N. S. Meldrum was vice president and general manager. Other directors included Sam Allen, James Appleby, Henry Brashear, John B. Dennis, Thomas C. Dunn, M. G. Howe, C. Lombardi, T. J. Groce, and James A. Baker, Jr. Of 19,200 shares of common stock outstanding, Jemison held 19,155 shares, and the others five shares each. New bonds bearing five percent interest for forty years to the amount of $3,840,000 were issued and were exchanged for the old first mortgage bonds. Other creditors were also satisfied, and the Union Trust Company of New York, to whom the property had been assigned at the time of the foreclosure purchase, conveyed the road back to the new HE&WT company on May 8, 1893.[1]

Elbert S. Jemison combined New York metropolitan experience with a Texas background. Born in Alabama, Jemison came to East Texas after he had completed his education and settled on a farm in Anderson County. During the Civil War he served in Hood's Brigade, where he was twice wounded and rose to the rank of captain. After the war he went to Galveston where he formed a partnership with W. S. Moody in the commission and cotton factor business. This company operated under a number of names, finally evolving into Jemison, Groce and Company. About 1875 the company established a branch office in New York, and Jemison took charge of the New York office. It is evident that Jemison knew Paul Bremond during these years for the "Builder" employed the New York branch of Moody and Jemison in a number of matters. It was only natural for the Union Trust Company to choose Jemison, because of his Texas contacts, to serve as their agent in the HE&WT foreclosure sale and subsequent reorganization. Also, because of this same Texas background it is not surprising that Jemison became interested in the HE&WT and welcomed the opportunity to acquire and operate the narrow-gauge road.[2]

The first task of the new company was to rehabilitate the road, and high on the priority list was the conversion of the entire line to standard-gauge. Only then would full interchange with connecting lines become possible and a considerable amount of transloading at the Shreveport and Houston terminals be avoided. For months before the changeover date the section crews worked to widen bridges and trestles and to replace six-foot ties with eight footers, the extra length extending to the west side of the road bed only. In the shops the machinists converted selected items of rolling stock to standard gauge and the company purchased eighteen new Rogers locomotives and 200 freight and passenger cars.[3]

At last, on July 29, 1894, the great day of the changeover came. One thousand men, including the regular section crews, casual workers, and convicts under guard, were divided into gangs and groups, each with a special task. According to one old-time railroad man, the actual track moving was accomplished after the regular passenger trains, each with narrow-gauge equipment, had passed each other a little south of Lufkin. Then working behind the trains, one group pulled the outside spikes from the left rail, the second group moved the freed rail into its new position without loosening a joint, and the third fastened the rail down temporarily by spiking every third tie. In the meantime, the group boss was busy with a spanner checking the gauge. By the end of the day the trains had completed their regular schedule and the job of changing the gauge was completed. The work trains, according to another veteran employee, had gone out that morning with narrow-gauge equipment carrying standard-gauge flat cars upside down, piggy back. When the job was completed the standard-gauge cars were placed on the tracks and the narrow-gauge cars rode home upside down, piggy back, on them. The next morning the passenger trains, this time with standard-gauge equipment, departed on schedule. The entire changeover had been accomplished in one working day at a cost of $300,000. The next month, the whole railroad family was invited to a fish fry at San Jacinto Springs to celebrate the event.[4]

The company purchased still more new rolling stock, full-size standard-gauge cars and coaches by Pullman and locomotives by Baldwin. The light thirty-five and forty-pound rails were replaced as rapidly as possible with sixty-pound rails. The old rails were sold for tram road use to the local lumber companies along the route. Four new steel bridges were erected across the San Jacinto, Trinity, Neches, and Sabine rivers, and a new wooden trestle 3248 feet long was built over the Angelina.[5] Apparently the new owners exerted every effort to put the "Bremond Road" in first class condition.[6]

In 1896 Elbert S. Jemison died and his widow, Louise Jemison, became for a brief time the principal stockholder. A second reorganization was effected in August of 1896, without foreclosure, in which $840,000 of first-mortgage bonds were cancelled. In the transaction, old bondholders received fifty-five percent new bonds and forty-five percent common stock of the value of the earlier bonds. Common stockholders lost ninety percent of their investments. The new president was T. W. House and the general manager was N. S. Meldrum. This same year the HE&WT was described as a Class I railroad of 192 miles, standard-gauge, with steel rails of 35-40-60 pounds on its main line. It had eighteen locomotives, eleven passenger cars, and 430 freight cars. The next year, 1897, it reported its earnings as: freight $254,395, and passenger $144,001. Net earnings were three times as great as the year before and road and equipment was valued at $4,920,000.[7]

The Louisiana portion of the system, the Houston and Shreveport, experienced only slightly different history. This road was released from receivership in December 1885, and continued to operate under its own management, including E. L. Bremond, until it defaulted on its bonds in the fall of 1889 and was again forced into receivership. M. G. Howe, who had served since 1885 as receiver for the HE&WT, became receiver for the H&S also and in this capacity operated the road until July 1891. At that time it was sold to Joseph Richardson and Marcus Hawley, who shortly conveyed it to a new Houston and Shreveport Railroad Company. The new company was headed by Jemison and included as stockholders and directors N. S. Meldrum, James H. Blair, R. S. Lovett, J. H. Jenkins, Frank N. Butler, and J. H. Shepherd, the last two from Louisiana. Like its Texas counterpart, the H&S was thoroughly rehabilitated and its gauge changed to standard on July 29, 1894. Evidently its earnings were greatly improved, for the directors declared and paid a one percent dividend in 1895.[8]

Although the HE&WT and the H&S were quite separate companies incorporated under the laws of different states, they had always operated as one line. In 1897 this relationship was made more specific by contract. They agreed on complete interchange of all traffic and pledged to send all business possible over the combined roads. Each allowed train crews to operate on the road of the other and employed the same crews. Costs were distributed pro rata on the basis of mileage: fuel, train supplies, construction and maintenance of bridges—except the upkeep on the Sabine River bridge, which was to be divided fifty percent to each road—as well as salaries of supervisory officials whose duties overlapped the two lines. The schedule for dividing revenues was as follows:

> Traffic originating at Livingston for Shreveport or beyond was divided 66/34; at Lufkin 56/44; at Nacogdoches 51/49; at Teneha 49/51.

On lumber shipped beyond Shreveport the division from Texas points allowed the H&S 2-1/2 cents out of a total of 7-1/2 cents per hundred charged. The next year the two companies contracted with the Western Union Telegraph Company to take over the 464 miles of wire along the 232 miles of HE&WT–H&S track and operate it for $500 per month. This rental was divided 5/6 and 1/6. In 1899 the Texas legislature authorized "Bremond's Road" to lease the H&S for a period of twenty-five years but did not include approval of consolidation, sale, or removal of the leased property. Apparently no application was made to the Louisiana legislature to lease the road. Under this arrangement the road was operated as one system until 1927.[9]

In the years following the second reorganization, the HE&WT acquired additional locomotives, coaches, and cars in order to serve its now rapidly increasing traffic. The freight earnings rose from $511,000 in 1897 to $685,000 in 1901. Passenger earnings increased from $99,000 to $226,000 during the same time.

Receipts from mail contracts, express, rents, and privileges increased the total annual earnings to nearly $1,000,000 by 1901. At long last the HE&WT was on a sound financial basis and was making money.[10]

The HE&WT had now become too valuable a property and occupied too strategic a position in the East Texas Piney Woods to remain an independent short line. Its direct route from Houston to Shreveport and the numerous feeder lines which connected with it gave "Bremond's Road" a great advantage in the contest to control the shipments of the Texas lumber industry which was just entering its bonanza period at the turn of the century. Within the next decade lumber production in the East Texas region rose to more than two billion board feet annually and a large part of the cut was shipped via the HE&WT.

In October 1899, the Southern Pacific Company acquired control of the HE&WT by purchasing substantially all of the outstanding common stock of the company, 19,064 out of 19,200 shares. At the same time the SP purchased $397,600 of the $400,000 worth of stock outstanding of the H&S. The main line of the SP ran east and west, from New Orleans, through Houston, San Antonio, and on to the west coast by way of El Paso. As it already owned the T&NO, the acquisition of the HE&WT gave the SP a network of roads, together with their feeders, through the Piney Woods. Eventually, in 1932, The Southern Pacific acquired the Cotton Belt, which made its East Texas network even more extensive.[11]

The Southern Pacific proceeded to again reorganize the road and to make further improvements in its rolling stock and right-of-way. Charles H. Tweed of New York became president of the HE&WT, and a new board of directors was chosen. Automatic couplers and airbrakes were installed and a second telegraph line was laid. The principal locomotive power was changed from wood to coal, and shortly thereafter from coal to oil. In every way the new managers sought to bring "Bremond's Road" up to the high standards of the SP main line.[12]

The HE&WT, as a Class I common carrier engaged in interstate commerce, was subject to the rules and regulations of the federal Interstate Commerce Commission, which had been established in 1887. At the same time, as a Texas-chartered railroad doing business in the state, the HE&WT was also under the regulation of the Texas Railroad Commission, established in 1891. Frequently these two regulating boards had opposing purposes and issued conflicting directives, both of which were binding on such a road as the HE&WT. One such controversial rate case involving "Bremond's Road" was the so-called "Shreveport Case." This case was eventually carried to the United States Supreme Court and became famous as a precedent for similar later litigation.

The Shreveport Case was the result of a long-standing and inequitable rate differential between freight shipped from Shreveport to Texas points and the same goods shipped a longer distance from Houston to the same points within Texas on the HE&WT. This discrimination was due to the control of intrastate traffic by the Texas Railroad Commission, while interstate traffic was regulated by the Interstate Commerce Commission in Washington. The ICC attempted to set fair and reasonable rates throughout the United States based on distance, class, and commodity schedules. The ICC had jurisdiction over all traffic moving across state lines, such as that from Shreveport to points on the HE&WT within the state of Texas. The Texas Railroad Commission, on the other hand, sought to pursue for the state a policy of "protection to its own industries." Its prescribed rates regularly were below the comparable rates in interstate commerce and the railroads thought that the Texas Commission was seeking to establish a policy which would make her "railroads within the State contribute in a manner believed by her own people to best subserve their own interests."[13]

In the first years after the HE&WT was completed, the Shreveport manufacturers and wholesale companies competed quite successfully for business with the Houston houses. Before the turn of the century the Shreveport drummer was as frequent a visitor at the Henderson and Kurth Lumber Company near Lufkin or a hardware company in Nacogdoches, for example, as was the drummer from Houston. Closer to Louisiana, in the villages of Garrison, Timpson, Teneha, and Joaquin, the Shreveport representative had a marked advantage in freight rates, and the merchants in these towns usually bought from Shreveport firms.[14]

By 1900, however, the Texas Railroad Commission had begun to systematically stipulate freight rates for the Texas towns along the HE&WT well below the rates available to Shreveport shippers under the Interstate Commerce Commission. For example, the first-class rate from Houston to Lufkin, a distance of 118 miles, was fifty cents per one hundred pounds, while the same rate from Shreveport to Lufkin, 112 miles, was sixty-nine cents. In Texas, the maximum rate was seven cents per hundred pounds on window glass from Houston; Shreveport, although it had a glass manufacturing plant, paid twenty-four cents per hundred on glass shipped to Texas.[15] Also there were many special commodity rates permitted by the Texas Commission, but only class rates, which were markedly higher, were available from Shreveport to Texas points.

As could be expected, the trade between Shreveport and the Texas towns along "Bremond's Road" slowly dried up. Shreveport houses that once had a dozen traveling men serving the East Texas trade, by 1910 had only three or four, and they were hard put to do enough business to justify their efforts. For example, the Henderson and Kurth Commissary by 1910 was buying almost entirely from Houston wholesale houses. The same could be said of sawmill companies all up and down the line.[16]

Faced with economic disaster, the City of Shreveport appealed to the Louisiana legislature for assistance in obtaining relief. The legislature appropriated $15,000 to carry the complaint to the ICC and employed competent counsel to present their case.[17] After considering the case for some two years the Commission at length handed down the decision which upheld the claims of the Shreveport shippers and ordered the HE&WT to "cease and desist from charging higher rates on any commodity from Shreveport into Texas than are contemporaneously charged for the carriage of such commodity from [Dallas and] Houston toward Shreveport for an equal distance."[18] This was the first time the ICC claimed power to interfere with state-established, intrastate rates which had a bearing on the interstate rates set by the Commission. The HE&WT promptly appealed the decision to the Commerce Court and when that body upheld the findings of the ICC, took the appeal to the Supreme Court of the United States.[19]

In a sweeping decision in the case of *Houston, East & West Texas Railway Company* v. *The United States*, the high court upheld the Commission on every count and dismissed the contention of the railroad. Speaking for the Court, Justice Charles Evans Hughes held that

> the fact that carriers are instruments of intrastate commerce, as well as of interstate commerce, does not deregate [sic] from the latter, or preclude the Federal power from being exerted to prevent the intrastate operations of such carriers from being made a means of injury to that which has been confided to Federal care. Whenever the interstate and intrastate transactions of carriers are so related that the government of the one involves the con-

> trol of the other, it is Congress, and not the state, that is entitled to prescribe the final and dominant rule, for otherwise Congress would be denied the exercise of its constitutional authority, and the state, and not the nation, would be supreme within the national field.[20]

There followed several years of litigation between the Texas Railroad Commission and the railroad companies which periodically appealed to the ICC for an order to enforce the interstate rates. Eventually, however, the Texas Railroad Commission, with some minor exceptions, regularly prescribed the interstate rates for intrastate traffic also. The long range results of the Shreveport Case was to transfer effective jurisdiction ever railroad rates from the state commission to the ICC. In its immediate effects, the Shreveport shippers regained their competitive position in regard to East Texas business, the Houston and Dallas manufacturers and jobbers were forced to compete without the benefit of a rate differential, and the HE&WT gained more equitable and profitable rates as well as a greater volume of business on the two-way haul.[21]

Except for the years during World War I when the federal government controlled all the railroads, the HE&WT continued to operate its properties under its own name until 1927. In that year it was leased to another SP affiliate, the Galveston, Harrisburg and San Antonio Railway. Seven years later both roads, together with the H&TC and a variety of short lines, were merged with the T&NO, which became the Southern Pacific operating company in Texas.[22] During these years the HE&WT became less and less identified with Paul Bremond and the struggling little narrow gauge of the late nineteenth century. It was no doubt less quaint, romantic, and picturesque, but it had become a much better railroad. “Bremond’s Road” had finally matured into a worthy Class I railroad and an important part of a great transcontinental system.

HE&WT engine number 34
courtesy Harry J. Heaney and Southern Pacific Company

VI

Connecting Lines

Connecting lines were, and still are, the veins and arteries of a railroad's traffic. The smaller roads brought lumber and cotton tonnage to the HE&WT from the more remote interior. Larger systems provided terminal facilities in Houston or Shreveport and valuable transfer points for the long and lucrative hauls of through traffic. Some were intimately related to the HE&WT and dependent upon it. Others were much more powerful, and "Bremond's Road" was in part dependent upon them. Altogether, the line of the HE&WT was crossed and crisscrossed by a great variety of railroads, some of them fearful and wonderful indeed.

At the time of the first track-laying in Houston the only connecting roads were the Texas and New Orleans; the Houston and Texas Central; the Galveston, Houston and Henderson; the International and Great Northern; and the Galveston, Harrisburg, and San Antonio. By the turn of the century or shortly afterward, the T&NO, the H&TC, and the GH&SA were all part of the Southern Pacific Lines. The main line of the Gulf, Colorado and Santa Fe had entered Houston, as had the Missouri, Kansas, and Texas, the Fort Worth and Denver City (Burlington), and the Rock Island

Lines. The I&GN had become part of the Missouri Pacific System, as had the Beaumont, Sour Lake and Western. In addition, for a time the Texas Western Narrow Gauge, the only road out of Houston with the same gauge as the HE&WT, ran westward to the cotton country. To this great transportation metropolis, the HE&WT provided the key to the resources of the Piney Woods. In addition it was the shortest route to the Northeast. It is not strange that the Southern Pacific system found this potentially valuable property desirable.[1]

As the road ran north from Houston, a branch line of the Gulf, Colorado, and Santa Fe crossed the HE&WT at Cleveland, running east and west. This road had originally been an independent short line called the Central and Montgomery Railway, extending from Navasota to Montgomery in the county of the same name. In 1882 it was acquired by President George Sealy and other Santa Fe officials who extended its western terminal to a connection with the GC&SF at Somerville and built it eastward to Conroe, a distance of seventy-four miles. Shortly afterward the parent company was itself acquired by the transcontinental Atchison, Topeka and Santa Fe, which welded the Texas road into its system. Yet another short line, the Texas, Louisiana & Eastern Railroad, had been chartered with headquarters at Conroe and in 1893 had built thirty miles through Cleveland to the Trinity River. Here it stopped, went into the hands of a receiver, and there languished until it was purchased by the Santa Fe in 1897. Five years later the TL&E was extended forty miles to Silsbee, where it linked up with another Santa Fe-controlled short-line, the Gulf, Beaumont and Kansas City.[2] The latter road had been chartered and built as far as Roganville by John Henry Kirby, the lumber tycoon, to provide transportation from Beaumont to his numerous sawmills situated in the heart of the Texas long-leaf belt. The acquisition of this line by the Santa Fe was mutually profitable to both parties. Kirby was primarily interested in lumbering and knew little about railroads. The Santa Fe had had great experience in building and operating railroads and was interested in the lumber traffic provided by the Kirby mills which the Santa Fe could route on its own lines to the Gulf, to West Texas, to the West Coast, and even to Chicago. With the completion and consolidation of these lines the AT&SF also penetrated the Piney Woods and assured for itself a substantial portion of the total cut of the region. In the immediate area of the Kirby mills the Santa Fe secured a near-monopoly of the traffic. This intimate relationship between John Henry Kirby and the Santa Fe continued for many years.[3]

At Livingston the HE&WT met the Waco, Beaumont, Trinity and Sabine Railway, a short line with an over ambitious name, whose tracks touched none of the places listed in its name except Trinity. In its career it had a variety of owners and a variety of names, but the local inhabitants usually referred to it by the rather uncomplimentary nickname "Wobblety, Bobblety, Turnover and Stop."[4] Others say the initials stand for "We Won't Be Back Till Saturday."

This road had its beginning as the Beaumont and Great Northern Railway, originally a tram road for a lumber company but chartered as a common carrier in 1905 by William Carlisle and Company. Carlisle was a lumber magnate who owned 140,000 acres of timber land and two large mills in East Texas with headquarters at Onalaska. Evidently this name intrigued him for according to local tradition he had previously owned a mill in Wisconsin, and later another in Arkansas by the name of Onalaska, and still later when he had cut out the timber in East Texas, he named a fourth mill Onalaska on the West Coast.

The B&GN ran from Trinity to Livingston, a distance of thirty-three miles, serving places with such exotic names as Sequoyah, Pegoda, Sebastopol, Luce, Carlisle, Onalaska, Kickapoo, Blanchard, Vreeland, and East Tempe. In 1905 the road was purchased by Colonel R. C. Duff, a Beaumont lawyer, who planned to build a railroad from Waco to Port Arthur via Beaumont using Carlisle's little road as a nucleus. However, Duff ran into financial difficulties and was forced to sell the road back to Carlisle. Next Duff conceived the idea of interesting the Missouri, Kansas, Texas Railroad in building a line from Waco through Beaumont to the Gulf. Carlisle agreed to sell the road back to Duff, including a new extension west from Trinity to Weldon, making a total of forty-eight miles. This transaction took place in 1912, and the same year Duff managed to sell the B&GN to the Katy, which shortly thereafter became involved in an antimonopoly suit and injunction with the attorney general of Texas over the property. This was not settled until 1914, when the MKT agreed to improve the entire property and connect the B&GN with the parent main line at Waco. The president of the MKT told his stockholders that he expected great benefits from this acquisition once the connection with the main line was built.[5]

Instead, the Katy went into receivership. Like some other roads in the Southwest, the Katy was overexpanded, overcapitalized, and, from their point of view, overregulated. The dislocation of traffic brought by the World War in 1914 and the simultaneous maturing of some $19,000,000 in short-term notes forced the default of the company. From 1915 to 1917 the B&GN was administered by the MKT receiver and then from 1917 to 1920 by the federal government. Finally, in 1923, the Katy reorganized and sloughed off unprofitable branch lines, including the B&GN. Duff, now for the third time, found himself in the railroad business again. He had also acquired for $100,000 the "Orphan Katy" running from Trinity to Colmesneil. He thereupon combined the two badly run-down pieces of track in a new company called the Waco, Beaumont, Trinity and Sabine Railway Company. Although Duff energetically made plans to extend his line to the Gulf Coast at Port Arthur and the Interstate

Commerce Commission approved the project in 1927, he was not able to complete the road. The decline of lumber traffic as the pine forests were cut out along the route and unfavorable divisions at both terminals forced the "Wobblety-Bobblety" into receivership in 1930. There it has remained. The "Orphan Katy" branch was abandoned in 1936 and the B&GN branch shortened its route materially during and immediately after World War II. Except for a part of the Weldon trackage, an eight-mile stretch from Trinity to Auburn in Walker County where there has been some oil field development, and a two-mile stub east of Trinity, the line has been abandoned and the rails taken up and sold for scrap. The charter has not been surrendered, but no trains have run since 1960, and the last rusting locomotive stands in the switchyard. Only a few old timers remember the "irregular" passenger service of its mixed freight and passenger train along the Livingston route in which the passenger rode in a long museum-piece combination coach and caboose, or the little Ford "rail-bus" which pulled a trailer as a "Jim Crow" car for Negro passengers. The WBT&S, despite its many shortcomings, held a warm spot in the hearts of many East Texans. Unfortunately, it never reached salt water at Sabine Pass.[6]

Another shortline which connected with the HE&WT at Livingston was the Livingston & Southeastern Railroad. This was chiefly a tram road running seven miles to the Knox Lumber Company, but it was chartered in 1903 and was recognized as a common carrier until 1913 when it abandoned operations. The president and principal stockholder was W. H. Knox, Sr., who had originally operated a mill in Wisconsin and whose son later built a large mill at Hemphill in Sabine County. Like other similar lines it was a welcome feeder of lumber and lumber products tonnage for the HE&WT.[7]

At Moscow the HE&WT intersected the Moscow, Camden & San Augustine Railroad, a lively little "cracker-barrel" road that as late as 1963 was still going strong. Moscow was already an old town when "Bremond's Road" first built through Polk County. Founded in 1846 by David Griggs Green, it was for a time known as Greenville and was recognized as a cultural and educational center of the region. According to some writers the name change came when the town got its first post office. Postal authorities denied the use of the name Greenville because of the prior claim of the Hunt County metropolis. A number of names were suggested and as regularly rejected until one of the village fathers disgustedly proposed Moscow. To his surprise it was approved. The citizens of Moscow had eagerly hailed the coming of the HE&WT and had cooperated in making donations of cash and land for trackage rights and station buildings which insured the passage of the line through the town.

The MC&SA was chartered in 1898 by the W. T. Carter and Brother Lumber Company. The year before, in 1897, the Carter mill at Barnum on the "Orphan" branch of the Missouri, Kansas, and Texas had burned and the brothers moved their operations to Camden. From Moscow seven miles of track was built in 1898 to the new mill at Camden but the line was never extended to its terminal at San Augustine as listed in the charter. At Camden the MC&SA was joined by the Carter Lumber Company tram road which in the past has been the principal means of transporting the log supply. It extended south to Camp Ruby in the southern part of Polk County and north to the Angelina River bottoms. The traffic of the road was largely lumber and lumber products, plus manufactured goods and food stuffs shipped in to the sawmill town of Camden from the HE&WT junction.

The rolling stock of the MC&SA originally consisted in part of castoff equipment from the HE&WT. When "Bremond's Road" changed to standard-gauge much of the stubby, narrow-gauge equipment was reworked to be used on the standard-gauge road. The cars and locomotives thus gave a bob-tailed appearance and were the subjects of numerous jokes. As rapidly as possible this renovated narrow-gauge equipment was sold to the short feeder or tram roads and new, more modern rolling stock was acquired for the main line. In the early years the standard mixed train of the MC&SA consisted of an ancient HE&WT ten-wheeler locomotive with wide tracks, several short, undersized box cars, also on standard tracks, and an old wooden combination baggage-passenger coach. Gradually the Carter officials replaced these items with more modern rolling stock, buying items from as widely scattered sources as the Panama Canal Zone, where the 2-6-0 "Mogul" locomotive had originally been adapted for a five-foot gauge, and the Long Island Railroad.

Steam locomotives still draw the heavily loaded freights and the colorful "mixed train daily." A bright red combine with a green roof and rattan seats that once carried commuters on Long Island rumbles through the closely wooded lowlands known as the "Big Thicket" between the HE&WT junction and the W. T. Carter Mill. Here six and eight yoke of oxen still compete with mules and tractors in drawing saw-logs to the rail or truck siding in an area that has been called the "wettest part of the world." Here also come rail fans and nostalgic visitors from all over the United States to ride once more through the Piney Woods behind the iron horse on the shortest main line in Texas. In more respects than one it is a run to yesteryear.[8]

At Corrigan the HE&WT crossed the notorious "Orphan Katy," a detached branch of the Missouri, Kansas, Texas Railway. The story how the Katy acquired this isolated and lonesome bit of track is one of the neatest examples of railroad skulduggery ever perpetrated. At one time Jay Gould, the great financier and railroad speculator, owned or controlled the MKT, the I&GN, and the Missouri Pacific. The I&GN running from Houston to Palestine needed a branch to tap the lumber region east of Trinity. To meet the need, local interests chartered the Trinity and

Sabine Railway in 1881 and began construction to Corrigan thirty-eight miles away. En route the T&S passed through White Rock; Saron; Groveton, location of the Joyce lumber interests; Saunders; Carmona; Willard, home of the Thompson and Tucker Lumber Company; and Corrigan. All of these were lumber towns of more or less importance. Indeed, it was said that a train passing along the route was never out of the sound of a sawmill whistle.[9]

This development was not of the slightest interest to the Katy, whose main line was one hundred miles to the west, at Temple and Waco. Yet Gould, by a "quick sleight of hand operation," bought this short line for the Missouri Pacific and the same day, December 9, 1882, sold it to the MKT. It isn't known what Gould paid for this thirty-eight mile logging road, but according to the biographer of the Katy, the MKT paid the MP $40,000 per mile. The MP continued to build this road through the Piney Woods until it reached Colmesneil, a village on the T&NO. And just as promptly Gould sold the additional mileage to the Katy. The MKT had no possible use for this branch line for it was entirely a feeder for the I&GN and the HE&WT, but its purchase was part of Gould's systematic looting of the Katy for the benefit of his other lines.[10]

Gould's control of the Katy and its Trinity-Corrigan branch ended in 1888, but the MKT continued to own and operate the "Orphan Katy" until after World War I. In the reorganization that followed a long receivership the Katy disposed of a number of lines, including the "Orphan." This branch, for which it had paid the MP $2,640,000, the MKT sold to Colonel R. C. Duff for $100,000. Under the name of Waco, Beaumont, Trinity and Sabine, the "Orphan Katy" continued to operate until 1936 by which time the timber had been cut out and the lumbermen had moved to more likely locations. As the local traffic could not sustain the road, the unfortunate orphan was abandoned that

Depot at Willard
courtesy East Texas Research Center

Thompson & Tucker Lumber Company engine
courtesy East Texas Research Center

year. The track was dismantled, and Corrigan, which had been an important junction point and interchange with the HE&WT, became once more merely a rural point on the line.[11]

At Diboll the HE&WT connects with the Texas South-Eastern Railroad owned by the Southern Pine Lumber Company. This short-line logging road with a common carrier charter pushes its way through the forests of Angelina and Trinity counties and finally rejoins "Bremond's Road" via the Cotton Belt at Lufkin, a distance of twenty-one miles.

According to the local tradition, Thomas Lewis Latané Temple, suitcase in hand, stepped off the HE&WT coach in the summer of 1893 and found himself in a small clearing in the midst of a pine thicket in southern Angelina County. Temple, a native of Virginia, had learned the lumber business in Texarkana, and now, at thirty-four, he was eager to build a lumber empire. He bought 7000 acres of timber from J. C. Diboll, a large land

T. L. L. Temple
courtesy East Texas Research Center

owner in the vicinity, and built his first sawmill. This was a small manually operated circular mill which blew its first whistle and ripped the first slab off a saw log before the end of 1894. From this modest beginning developed the complex of Temple Industries which today are among the largest and most comprehensive manufacturers of lumber and lumber products in the United States. Branches of the parent enterprise include the Southern Pine Lumber Company, Temple Lumber Company, Temple Manufacturing Company, Temple-White Company, Love Wood Products of Texas, Temple Associates, Temple Steel Products Company, Temple Associates Box Factory, Temple Builders Supply, and the Texas South-Eastern Railroad.[12] The companies are now operated by the third and fourth generation of the Temple family.

In 1900, when the TS-E was first chartered, the road ran east of Diboll and opened up the timber stands in the Neches River bottoms. By 1908 the timber east of Diboll had been cut out and the Temple Company abandoned this track. The line was extended westward across the Neches River to Vair in Trinity County and a logging spur was run into Houston County. A branch ran from Blix, seven miles west of Diboll, to Lufkin and the junction with the Cotton Belt. Over these tracks also ran the Groveton, Lufkin and Northern, chartered in 1908 by the Joyce lumber interests, which built twenty-one miles of track from Groveton to Vair and secured trackage rights on the TS-E into Lufkin. This gave Joyce alternate outlets for his lumber on the HE&WT or the Cotton Belt. This line was abandoned in 1931. Until a relatively few years ago the TS-E operated a mixed train daily pulled by a venerable iron horse. Among the local citizens the roads initials came to stand for "Tattered, Shattered and Expired." More recently the passenger service has been discontinued, and a powerful new diesel pulls the trains of finished lumber products. The old steam locomotive now is on exhibition in an open air museum in Diboll.[13]

The HE&WT crossed a major railroad at Lufkin where it met the Cotton Belt. Like most of the Texas shortlines this branch had a varied and interesting history, as well as a variety of names. It began as a locally controlled, narrow-gauge road constructed in 1877 from Tyler north to give that city a rail connection with the Texas and Pacific at Big Sandy. This was called the Tyler Tap Railroad. About the same time another local road, the Rusk Transportation Company, secured a charter to connect that town via Jacksonville with Tyler. Four years of work exhausted their resources and produced only a rickety, narrow-gauge line with wooden rails as far as Jacksonville. Rolling stock consisted of a single donkey engine and a few decrepit cars. This was sold in 1881 to a new company, the Kansas and Gulf Short Line, which built a narrow-gauge road south from Tyler and rehabilitated the wooden rail section between Jacksonville and Rusk. It too went into receivership but was bailed out for a time by the Texas & St. Louis Railway of Texas (later the St. Louis, Arkansas and Texas Railway), which became part owner of the property and provided the money to extend the road to Lufkin, a distance of forty-four miles.

The K&GSL reached Lufkin in 1885, making that city a junction town. Like the HE&WT it was a narrow-gauge road and depended principally upon lumber and lumber products for its traffic. Along its route were the sawmills of the Henderson and Kurth Lumber Company, the Clawson Lumber Company, and the Chronister Lumber Company, as well as the fabulous but ephemeral New Birmingham. This town, now disappeared, was built about 1883 to exploit the iron ore that was abundant in the region. New Birmingham was backed in part by British capitalists who developed it into a city of over 3,000 population, boasting brick buildings, electric lights, a newspaper, and a street railway. At its peak the New Birmingham blast furnaces produced an estimated 50,000 tons of pig iron annually. Inferior fuel, unfavorable freight rates in comparison with eastern steel companies, and the withdrawal of the British investors, thanks in part to the Texas Alien Land Law, spelled the doom of New Birmingham, and the furnaces were shut down and the town abandoned. Today the foundations of the furnaces and a few buildings are all that are left of the one time "Pittsburgh of East Texas."[14]

The arrival of the K&GSL and its junction with the HE&WT quickened the growth of Lufkin and produced a big celebration and land sale in the summer of 1885. Both lines ran summer excursions which were popular with the young men of the region but which led conservative citizens to complain of the "fights and rowdyism" in Lufkin due to the excursionists. The HE&WT took advantage of the new junction point and soon advertised that their trains made direct connections with the K&GSL. For example, a newspaper notice in 1891 read:[15]

Always on Time
HOUSTON EAST & WEST TEXAS RAILWAY
Connects at Shreveport with
Q&C; T&P; and St.LA&T Ry.
Connects in Lufkin with the
St.LA& [K&GSL]
Connects in Houston with H&TC,
and S. Pacific Ry.; and GC&SF Ry.
without layover.
20 minutes in Timpson for supper.

No. 1		No. 11	
Leaves Houston	8:30 A.M.	Leaves Shr'port	6:00 A.M.
Leaves Lufkin	3:40 P.M.	Arrives Nacog.	11:10 A.M.
Arrives Tyler	5:30 P.M.	Leaves Tyler	7:00 A.M.
Arrives Nacog.	4:47 P.M.	Leaves Lufkin	12:40 P.M.
Arrives Shr'port	10:00 P.M.	Arrives Houston	8:00 P.M.

Sleeping cars from Shreveport to points North and East.

M. G. Howe, Receiver — R. S. Collins, G.P.A.

In 1889 the K&GSL and the St.LA&T were forced once again into receivership and were purchased at a foreclosure sale by the St. Louis Southwestern Railway, more popularly known as the Cotton Belt. This gave the Houston and Lufkin travelers a direct connection with a line that would carry them into St. Louis in its own cars and on its own tracks. In Nacogdoches, citizens who were irritated at the slow service of the HE&WT and the poor connections out of Shreveport proposed that the people of the town could profitably build "a few miles of track and a bridge across the Angelina River to connect with the Cotton Belt."[16] This however, was not done.

In 1900 a logging road was chartered as a common carrier, with headquarters in Lufkin, under the name of the Texas and Louisiana Railroad. This was built to serve the properties of the Lufkin Land and Lumber Company and eventually reached White City, a point on the T&NO. This too, was acquired by the Cotton Belt, giving it a total of 128 miles of track south of Tyler. In the 1930s, after the timber had been cut out and the lumber companies ceased to exist, the Cotton Belt abandoned the trackage east of Lufkin.[17]

The Cotton Belt itself was acquired by the Southern Pacific in 1932 though the road continued to operate under its own name and organization. Thus the HE&WT and the K&GSL

became after many years partners in the same system. The rowdies who battled in the streets of Lufkin while awaiting rival excursions back in the 1890s would have never believed it!

Just north of Lufkin the HE&WT crossed the Angelina & Neches River Railroad. Like many of the other connecting lines, the A&NR was essentially a logging road for the Angelina County Lumber Company but was also chartered as a common carrier. The A&NR operated from Keltys on the Cotton Belt and extended east and north through Herty, the home of the Southland Paper Mills. It intersected the T&NO at Dunagan Station, bridged the Angelina River on a treated pine trestle, and passed through Etoile before reaching its terminal at Chireno, a small village near the Attoyac River. Chartered in 1900 and completed in 1912, the A&NR ran a "mixed train daily" until 1952, hauling miscellaneous freight to the villages in the Piney Woods, the few passengers riding in a coach or a caboose. During the depression of the 1930s, the road ran a motor coach on rails to accommodate passengers.

Avoiding interference with the "main line" train, a logging train used the same tracks en route to sidings deep in the forests where mules, tractors, and trucks brought sufficient logs to trackside to make a trainload in the course of a day's work. Time was when the logging was done by means of spur lines built out from the tap line into the woods and the logs brought to trackside by means of steam skidders. This practice was abandoned by the lumber company, however, to avoid needless destruction of the forests and to encourage the development of the young trees. A typical logging train on the A&NR consisted of twenty cars of logs, powered by a steam locomotive with the train crew and loaders riding in an ancient "crummy" (caboose). The running time from the siding at Etoile to Keltys consumed one to one and one-half hours in comparison with a half hour from the same location by truck or car.[18]

Steam skidder loading logs
courtesy East Texas Research Center

Overseeing an empire that includes not only the A&NR and the Angelina County Lumber Company but substantial interests in the Southland Paper Mills, the Lufkin National Bank, the Lufkin Foundry, and assorted other lumber interests, was Ernest L. Kurth, Jr. Preceding him had been his father, Ernest L. Kurth, Sr., and his grandfather, Joseph H. Kurth. The original founder of the dynasty, according to his own account, arrived in Galveston in 1878 from Germany with little except his own abilities to serve him and went to work as a day laborer in a Galveston sawmill. In 1887 he purchased a small mill at Keltys, and at his death four decades later the nucleus of the vast fortune had been already accumulated and was passed on to his heirs intact.[19]

The A&NR became a prosperous and profitable enterprise thanks to heavy traffic originating at the Angelina County Lumber Company in Keltys and the Southland Paper Mills in Herty,

Angelina County Lumber Company engine at Poe Lake Crossing
courtesy Museum of East Texas Collection. Gift of Jay Morrison.

as well as the foundries in Lufkin. In addition it served the needs of the Angelina County Lumber Company for a logging road and provided a needed freight service to and from villages and towns in the Piney Woods. When the region is tied together more fully by highways, this need to some points may disappear and the freight trains to such points might also be abandoned. But a part at least of the road will remain, due to its very considerable lumber and paper products traffic, a valuable feeder to the HE&WT and the Southern Pacific System, including the St. Louis Southwestern Railway Lines.[20]

In 1903 the Texas and New Orleans Railroad completed its branch from Beaumont to Dallas, intersecting the HE&WT at Nacogdoches. This pioneer Texas railroad, which had completed an east-west line from Houston to the Sabine before the Civil War, passed under the control of Collis P. Huntington of the

Southern Pacific in 1881. When it was determined to tap the Piney Woods and connect Beaumont and Sabine Pass with Dallas, the T&NO acquired existing short lines and constructed additional track connecting them. The Sabine and East Texas Railway was admirably suited for this purpose and Huntington purchased it from local interests in Kountze in 1882 and assigned it to the T&NO. This line was extended north and west from Rockland, crossing the A&NR at Dunagan Station and connecting, in 1902, with the HE&WT at Dorr Junction, on the outskirts of Nacogdoches. It had been the original intention of the T&NO to run its own tracks through the town, crossing Bremond's Road north of the business section, and a partial right-of-way was actually thrown up. The town fathers protested strenuously, however, and as the two lines by this time were both owned by the Southern Pacific, the T&NO went through Nacogdoches on the HE&WT tracks, separating again at Banita Junction, five miles to the north.[21]

In the meantime the Southern Pacific acquired another short line that extended from Dallas through Kaufman to Cedar (now Gossett). This was called the Texas Trunk Railroad, chartered in 1879, and said to have had more receivers than any railroad in Texas.[22] Title passed to the Southern Pacific in 1895, which assigned it to the T&NO two years later. Under the new management, construction from Cedar to Jacksonville was completed by the summer of 1902, and the final link between Banita Junction and Jacksonville, via two new villages en route bearing the inverted names Sacul (Lucas) and Reklaw (Walker) named for prominent land owners along the route, in May 1903.[23]

The Texas and New Orleans was a sizable railroad even before it was taken over by the Southern Pacific, and eventually it was chosen as the company which held and operated all of the SP lines in Texas, including the HE&WT. The completion of the Beaumont-Dallas branch was a great boon to the towns along the right-of-way and to the merchants of Nacogdoches, where all talk of building a connecting branch to the Cotton Belt ceased. Though they continued to operate as separate lines until the merger in 1934, the HE&WT and T&NO complemented each other's territory and provided a profitable division of traffic. Like most railroads the T&NO acquired a variety of nicknames. To the local citizens along the route it was popularly referred to as "the Wooden Axle Road." Newspaper reporters named it "Time No Object." Others called it "the Turnips and New Onions," while some coined names even less complimentary. Like the connecting lines discussed in this chapter, the T&NO opened up new areas of the Piney Woods to the saw mills and logging camps. Perhaps it was appropriate that most of these roads should eventually become one system.[24]

At Nacogdoches the HE&WT was joined by a quaint little road called the Nacogdoches & Southeastern, which extended eastward forty-two miles to a point named Calgary on the Santa Fe. This was essentially a logging and lumber hauling road owned successively by the E. B. Hayward Lumber Company, the Frost-Johnson Lumber Company, the Frost Lumber Industries, and the Olin Industries, Inc., which companies owned in turn a large sawmill in Nacogdoches and thousands of acres of timber land in the Attoyac watershed. The road was begun in 1903 but received its charter as a common carrier in September 1905. From a simple depot in Nacogdoches the N&SE made its way to the mill and then east and southeast along a grade thrown up in 1888 by the Red River, Sabine and Western Railway, which planned to build a trunk line from the Gulf to Denver. This company exhausted its funds, however, and the charter lapsed, leaving ten miles of grade which was badly overgrown by the time the N&SE began construction. The road passed through Woden, a forest village known chiefly for an avid basketball team, and on to Oil Springs, the location of one of the earliest oil wells in Texas and the site in

1867–1868 of Texas' first oil boom.[25] From Oil Springs a company-owned logging road extended south and east to La Cerda, where it crossed the A&NR and on to the dense timber thicket at the confluence of the Angelina and Attoyac. Here a large lumber camp, called Camp Pershing, was established during the First World War. From Pershing the N&SE served spur lines which extended in many directions. The Frost Company, as well as its predecessor, logged with rehaul steam skidders and loaders which were efficient in getting the lumber out but very damaging to young trees. More than 100,000 acres, much of it served by the N&SE, were logged out by the Frost Company in this manner. In many areas the scars are still to be seen.

From Oil Springs the main line was extended in 1923–1925 east and north across the Attoyac to Calgary on the Santa Fe. This new track, twenty-eight miles long, was also built by the Frost Lumber Company and leased to the N&SE. As the timber had been cut out along the old line the main lumber camp was relocated, this time near the Attoyac River at a place called Camp Worth and the buildings at Pershing were moved. From Camp Worth the timber along the upper Attoyac was logged.[26]

The N&SE carried many commodities besides lumber. It hauled foodstuffs, fertilizer, supplies, garden produce, cotton, cattle, and even automobiles into and out of the Piney Woods. Its equipment included four small engines, two passenger coaches, and assorted cars and cabooses. Each day two mixed trains plied their way between Nacogdoches and Calgary through the very heart of the Piney Woods. Negro sawmill bands sang a song that went:

> Oh that train—
> That Southeastern passenger train!
> I'm gonna buy me a ticket
> as long as my arm,

I'm gonna ride that train
all night long!
Oh that train—
That Southeastern passenger train![27]

The N&SE discontinued passenger service soon after 1928 and dropped scheduled runs at the same time. It continued operating as a lumber and general freight hauling railroad until 1954, when its physical properties were sold to the Southern Pacific and the road was abandoned. Unlike most short lines, the N&SE was a profitable venture. It had always operated in the black and made money.[28]

Another short line joined the HE&WT at Timpson. This was the Timpson Northwestern Railway, later renamed the Timpson and Henderson, which extended across Rusk County to Henderson, where it linked up with a branch line of the I&GN. This was essentially a logging road, owned by the Ragley-Saner Lumber Company, but it was chartered and recognized as a common carrier in 1901 and carried general freight and passengers. Like most of the other short lines it ran a "mixed train daily" through the Piney Woods. Although the T&H provided a feeder line for the HE&WT, it furnished an important alternate route for the shipment of lumber and lumber products for the Ragley-Saner Lumber Company. It continued operation until 1923, when the timber supply was depleted and the saw mill ceased operation. The railroad was abandoned the same year.[29]

The East Texas branch of the Santa Fe crossed the HE&WT again at Teneha. In acquiring the several short lines necessary to make this connection, the Santa Fe found itself in possession of a complex of roads with a varied history. In 1877 the Longview and Sabine Valley was chartered to build to the Gulf. Successively under the names of the Galveston, Sabine and St. Louis Railway; the Texas, Sabine Valley and Northwestern; and the Texas and Gulf, the road was extended southward to Carthage which was reached in 1885. Another line, the Marshall, Timpson and Sabine Pass Railroad, was built from Carthage south to Gary and Timpson in 1896.[30] These roads were consolidated in 1904 under the name of Texas & Gulf, and the next year the Santa Fe gained legislative approval to purchase the T&G over the governor's veto. Shortly thereafter the Timpson line was extended eighteen miles to Grigsby, a tiny village in southern Shelby County, and in 1908 the twenty-one mile gap between the T&G and the GB&KC was filled by the construction of a line from Gary to Center, crossing "Bremond's Road" at Teneha. Thus the Santa Fe completed its East Texas branch line which tapped the Piney Woods and provided an alliance with lumber tycoon John Henry Kirby. It extended from the main line at Somerville via Conroe, Cleveland, Kountze, and Silsbee, where another branch went to Beaumont and High Island, Kirbyville, San Augustine, Center, Carthage, and Longview, crossing the HE&WT twice en route. Originally it was intended to complete the branch to rejoin the Santa Fe main line at Paris but this track was never built.[31]

After crossing the Sabine at Logansport the HE&WT, or more accurately its H&S affiliate in Louisiana, proceeded on its way to the terminal in Shreveport without interruption except for an occasional tram road crossing. At Shreveport it made connection with the Texas and Pacific, another branch of the Cotton Belt, the Shreveport and Red River, and the Kansas City Southern.

The Kansas City Southern, or "Casey," almost became intimately involved in the history of "Bremond's Road." In the late 1880s, a Kansas City business man, Arthur E. Stilwell, who already was part owner of a local suburban railroad, conceived the idea of building an "air line" railroad to the Gulf. His plan was to build to Shreveport and to use the HE&WT as a connection to Houston and Galveston. Before the KCS reached Shreveport Stilwell learned that the Houston to Shreveport road had been foreclosed and was for sale. He hurried to New York and secured an option to purchase it. Then he had a hunch. According to his own account, he became possessed of an overpowering fear that "we were planning wrongly this time in relying on the Coast of the Gulf of Mexico as our principal terminus because of the storms of tremendous violence that lashed these shores at times."

Instead he envisioned a city located on a landlocked lake, safe from the most devastating storm the Gulf could produce, connected with the Gulf by means of a canal. Here he could build grain elevators, warehouses, piers and docks, and establish a port for the shipment of wheat from Kansas and the other grain states. Consequently he and his directors passed up the HE&WT deal and instead purchased facilities on Sabine Lake, laid out a town called Port Arthur, built a canal to deep water, and promoted the sale of adjoining land to a colony of Dutch rice farmers. The KCS, when constructed, first touched Texas briefly at Texarkana, ran down the western edge of Louisiana, and reentered Texas near Orange. Port Arthur enjoyed a flourishing grain trade for a number of years, and when the discovery at Spindletop blew in the Texas oil boom, Stilwell's city became a leading refinery and oil export center. Thus, by the margin of a "hunch" did the HE&WT miss becoming part of the "Casey" system instead of the "Espee."[32]

The Houston connections gave the HE&WT outlets to the west, Gulf Coast, and sea-borne traffic. The Shreveport terminal provided routes to the north, northwest, and east. The short lines, cracker barrel routes, and branch line crossings gave "Bremond's Road" a network of feeder lines and valuable interchange of traffic. The whole network provided a system of railways which opened up every section of the Piney Woods. And the heart of the network was the HE&WT.

VII

"The Rabbit"

The HE&WT became for a time a most notorious and celebrated road. Perhaps not so famous as the Atchison, Topeka, & Santa Fe, which broke all records in 1905 as it hurtled "Death Valley Scotty" from the West Coast to Chicago in the Coyote Special. Nor yet so celebrated as the Southern Pacific which won a famous victory over Jay Gould himself in the much publicized "joint track" controversy. Nor even as famous as one of Gould's roads, the Wabash, which is still remembered as whiskey tenors tell of the last run of the "Wabash Canonball." But there have been songs, and stories written about Bremond's Road which have traveled across the country, and often have been appropriated by raconteurs and applied to whatever bedraggled short line was well known in that region.

Long before its tracks reached the Sabine the HE&WT had acquired a nickname that stuck with it for more than thirty years. Because of its short, bobbing, narrow-gauge cars, its up and down hill roadbed, its "out of breath" puffer belly engines, its tendency to jump the track, and above all its proclivity for "stopping behind every stump," the road was promptly labeled "The Rabbit." And "The Rabbit" it remained for more than a generation. It is ironic that the farmers and businessmen along the route, the very people who were most eager for "Bremond's Road" to build through their county or town, were the first to denounce the line's shortcomings and to deride the narrow gauge and its antiquated equipment. If the train on a given date was woefully late, the word would be passed around among the crowd at the depot that "the Rabbit has jumped the track again." If the train pulled in on time, some wag would convulse the "boys" with the observation that this was "yesterday's train."

In an era in which all railroads were nicknamed and the initials in their names were given as bizarre a translation as possible, it was perhaps inevitable that the HE&WT was given a tagline that became famous throughout the country. The HE&WT, as it was said, was the perfect example of the traveling salesman's nightmare—"Hell Either Way Taken."[1] Perhaps it was. With the sway resulting from its narrow gauge base, and the pitch built into its short tracks and rough roadbed, plus the hand brakes and manual couplings which prevailed until the turn of the cen-

"The Rabbit" at Lufkin
courtesy Harry J. Heaney

tury, the drummer must most certainly have looked upon any extended trip on "Bremond's Road" with foreboding.

Others, particularly employees, insisted that the initials stood for something quite different: "How Easy We Travel." According to O. R. Estes, old time agent on the HE&WT, the people along the route were often so eager to take a trip on the railroad that the countryside was all but depopulated when an excursion came through. Once, back in 1909, "Bremond's Road" ran an excursion out of Houston to Shreveport for the Ringling Brothers Circus. All along the line crowds of people welcomed the holiday train, and at Timpson, sixty-five miles from Shreveport, 500 people bought tickets at seventy-five cents each per round trip. When the train pulled in, the conductor told the agent that he couldn't take his passengers, for excursionists "were stacked up three deep in the aisles then." Just then the engineer walked up and asked the problem. When told he turned to the agent and asked if he had any boxcars. There were three and these were hitched on the excursion and the Timpson passengers climbed in and went to the circus. "How Easy We Travel"—in boxcars.[2]

The Piney Woods abounded in stories concerning events and exploits along the route of the HE&WT. There was the tale of the green engineer who didn't notice that the Santa Fe switch at Cleveland was open and "highballed" some fifty miles along the Santa Fe road to Kountze before be realized that he had strayed from his own line. There was the story of the novice agent who spent an hour looking for the green oil for the green lantern and the red oil for the red lantern after he had been told to keep the lamps well filled with the proper oil. Then there was the derailment of a "Rabbit" locomotive at Moscow, whereupon the bull team from the Carter Lumber Company logging operation nearby was brought in to help nudge the engine back on the track. Also there was the story of the tramp, probably mythical, who hopped a ride on the "blinds" on a HE&WT passenger train south from

Shreveport. After about a hundred miles he pulled the emergency cord that stopped the train. When the conductor came back to investigate, the tramp stood up and dusted himself off with an air of indignation. He said that he had planned to ride to Houston but be couldn't take it anymore. It was too rough! He would rather walk!

Captain I. L. Sturdevant of Nacogdoches related an exciting experience which occurred in the late 1880s. Captain Sturdevant at that time was a young cotton buyer and commission merchant with headquarters at Climax, a settlement on the HE&WT five or six miles south of Nacogdoches, but north of the Angelina River. One summer evening he was returning on foot along the HE&WT track from a trip to Lufkin where he had delivered some receipts and other records. By the time he reached the Angelina River it was dark but a half-moon gave him sufficient light to walk the trestle without difficulty. All went well until he neared the Nacogdoches side. Then suddenly he found his way barred by a snarling wildcat—it looked as big as a mountain lion at the time!—which gave no indication of backing up but was evidently intent on crossing the river on the trestle himself. The two stood there eyeing each other for what seemed thirty minutes, neither giving an inch, with Sturdevant unarmed except for a small bag of groceries which he had brought from Lufkin. Then in the distance he heard the whistle of an approaching northbound freight train as it cleared the last of the river hills and blew for the Angelina crossing. Sturdevant took a couple of steps forward but was driven back by the bared teeth and angry snarl of the cat. Here was a dilemma. The cat evidently had not heard the approaching locomotive, and it was already too late for him to recross the trestle. Shortly a second whistle signaled that the train was on the trestle and a long beam of light from its headlamp showed both man and cat in sharp silhouette. The beam caught the cat's eyes and the light danced in unbridled savage fury. By this time the roar of the drive shafts and the sound of the wheels under the heavy cars came across the bridge, and the weight of the train made the trestle tremble. Sturdevant started forward again. The cat hesitated, then with a final snarl, turned and dived from the side of the trestle into the tree tops on the side of the right of way. Sturdevant, with a sigh of relief, scrambled down the trestle a few yards toward solid ground and jumped off on the opposite side just before the "Rabbit" steamed by at the speed of twenty miles per hour. It was a hair-raising experience, but except for a few bruises and scratches, and the loss of his bag of groceries, he was none the worse for the incident. But it was a long time before Captain Link Sturdevant made such a trip again unarmed.[3]

The HE&WT was the locale of the cry made internationally famous by crapshooters seeking to make the point of ten. Like "Eighter from Decatur, the County Seat of Wise," for the eight shooters, those trying for the big double fives would call out "Ten-aha, Timpson, Bobo, and Blair." All of these are communities in Shelby County on the HE&WT. Tenaha and Timpson are considerable towns, while Bobo and Blair were very small places that at present have virtually disappeared, but all were significant settlements at the turn of the century. One resident of the Timpson area insists that the cry began in a National Guard unit before World War I. Most of the soldiers in the company were from northern Shelby County, and they began the habit of shouting their home towns instead of the usual hup, two, three, four. Because of the rhythm it came out "Teneha, Timpson, Bobo, and Blair." Dice players took it up, and the soldiers in the war spread the expression far and wide. Still another version has it that a Negro porter in the Houston station became an accomplished train caller and frequently was tipped by local citizens just to hear his melodious chant of stations, large and small, up the line of the Houston, East and West Texas Railway. One of his favorite sequences was "Tenaha, Timpson, Bobo and Blair," which was repeated frequently for excursion runs and specials. The phrase was taken up by the soldiers, dice shooters, and others, and hence spread.[4]

The East Texas folk singer, Tex Ritter, became famous singing a comedy hit song with the title of "Tenaha, Timpson, Bobo and Blair." The song had little to do with the narrow gauge that was "Bremond's Road" but it spread the names of the four small villages far and wide. A few of the more official verses are as follows:

Tenaha, Timpson, Bobo and Blair

Music by Dan Beaty

Whistle in the Piney Woods

1. On that HE—WT Line
Old East Texas sure looks fine.
Drop me off just anywhere (near)
Tenaha, Timpson, Bobo, and Blair.

2. Hear those drivers pound the rails
Takin' me back to Texas trails.
Bought my ticket, paid my fare (to)
Tenaha, Timpson, Bobo and Blair.

Chorus:

Whooooo, waiting for the whistle,
Whooooo, when you hear the whistle
It means that the station's not so far
from where we are.

Monologue:

Red clay and piney woods
Sabine river, trot lines
Catfish and goggle eyes
Brown mule and Star Navy
ham gravy
Levi Garrett, won't bat
Brush arbor meetin's and dinner on the ground
Sacred harp singin', shaped notes
Choppin' in high cotton
Eatin' high on the hog
Plowin' the new ground
Butter in the well, on the north side
Box cars and snake eyes
Eighter from Decatur and Little Joe
Baby needs a new pair of shoes
Tenaha, Timpson, Bobo and Blair

Chorus:

Whoooooo, waiting for the whistle
Whoooooo, when you hear the whistle
It means the station's not so far
from where we are

3. Let 'er highball, engineer.
Pull that throttle, track is clear.
There's a gal just waitin' there (in)
Tenaha, Timpson, Bobo and Blair.[5]

The HE&WT opened up the Piney Woods region of East Texas. Along its route grew up flourishing towns, thriving industries, and improved homes. In its cars, derided and ridiculed though they were in the early days, lay the only route to the outside world and to the city. The building of the HE&WT and its connecting lines to a large extent made possible the commercial lumber industry in East Texas, and along the route of "Bremond's Road" were to be found the plants of most of the big names in Texas lumber. The Carters, Temples, Kurths, Knoxes, Haywards, Frosts, Thompsons, Ragleys, Saners, and Pickerings all built their mills near its right-of-way and shipped their lumber on its cars. They supplied the principal traffic; the HE&WT supplied the transportation.

The HE&WT also provided place names for much of the region. Along the route Cleveland, Shepherd, Goodrich, Corrigan, Burke, Lufkin, Appleby, Fitze, Meldrum, Blair, and Timpson were all named for HE&WT personalities. In the towns and cities along the route, almost all have a street named Bremond and many have a street called Groesbeck.

Some nights when the December wind blows from the south and the full moon shines down upon the forests, perhaps in fancy one can still catch the rhythmic click of the wheels over the light rails of the narrow gauge, can hear the groan of a heavily loaded freight as it clears the last of the river hills, and can find oneself listening for the lonesome wail of the "Rabbit's" locomotive as it whistles for the Angelina crossing. The sound of the whistle echoes in the stillness of the Piney Woods. This was the dream that obsessed Paul Bremond as the spirit of Moseley Baker drove him to build the HE&WT. This was the "Whistle in the Piney Woods" that signaled progress and civilization to the East Texas region. Despite frustrations and delays, the dream at last came true.

Notes

I. Mr. Bremond

[1]Association of American Railroads, *American Railroads, Their Growth and Development* (Washington, 1954), 3–6.

[2]Ibid., 17–22; John F. Stover, *The Railroads of the South, 1865–1900* (Chapel Hill, 1955), 3–14; George Rogers Taylor and Irene D. Neu, *The American Railroad Network, 1861–1890* (Cambridge, Mass., 1956), 1–7.

[3]St. Clair G. Reed, *A History of the Texas Railroads* (Houston, 1941), 124; *Texas Almanac, 1958–59* (Dallas, 1959), 292. Other roads included the Eastern Texas (from Beaumont to Sabine Pass), the San Antonio and Mexican Gulf (from Victoria to Port Lavaca), and the Southern Pacific (no relation to the Huntington road), which operated a short stretch of track in the Marshall, Shreveport area.

[4]Frank H. Taylor, "Through Texas," *Harper's Monthly,* 59:706 (1879). *Houston Telegraph,* May 9, 1879; *Burke's Almanac, 1880* (Houston, 1880), 66–73; Reed, *Texas Railroads,* 746.

[5]Albert Hanford, ed., *Texas State Register and Almanac, 1876* (Houston, 1876); Taylor, "Through Texas," 706. On the Eastern Texas Railroad see also the Bennett Blake papers in the Stephen F. Austin State University Library, Nacogdoches, Texas.

[6]Reed, *Texas Railroads,* 67–83. Bremond also had been a stockholder in the Houston Tap and Brazoria Railway.

[7]"Mayo Manuscript," Southern Pacific Papers. Southern Pacific Lines, Houston, Texas; Reed, *A History of Texas Railroads,* 69–71; H. Bailey Carroll, *Standard History of Houston* (Knoxville, Tennessee, 1912), 239–40; Louis Kemp, "Sketch of Paul Bremond," n.d., (manuscript in possession of Mrs. Edith Bremond Koch, Houston, Texas.)

[8]Interview with Mrs. Edith Bremond Koch, October 30, 1958, Houston, Texas; "Plat Map," Glenwood Cemetery, Houston, Texas; Dr. S. O. Young, *Thumb-Nail History of Houston* (Houston, 1912), 65–69.

[9]*Houston Post,* May 16, 1885; *Houston Chronicle,* December 30, 1939; Young, *Thumb-Nail History,* 69–70; Kemp, "Sketch of Paul Bremond."

II. Opening the Piney Woods

[1]"Minute Book, no. 1, HE&WT Ry.," Southern Pacific Papers, Houston, Texas; Reed, *Texas Railroads,* 236–37.

[2]H. P. N. Gammel, *The Laws of Texas (*10 vols., Austin, 1898), VIII: 676–81; "Minute Book, HE&WT Ry.," Southern Pacific Papers, Houston Texas; Reed *Texas Railroads,* 236. Timpson was not listed as an incorporator in the ACT as reported by Gammel.

[3]*Houston Telegraph,* April 9, 1875. The legislature chartered two narrow gauge roads with headquarters in Houston about the same time. The other was the Western Narrow Gauge or Texas Western Narrow Gauge which had ambitions to run west to El Paso. Reed, *Texas Railroads,* 478, 530–40.

[4]*Houston Telegraph,* July 6, 1876.

[5]"Journal No. 1, HE&WT Ry., June 16, 1876," Southern Pacific Papers.

[6]"Journal No. 1, HE&WT Ry., December 15, 1877," Southern Pacific Papers.

[7]"Journal No. 1, HE&WT Ry., 1876–1882," Southern Pacific Papers; *Houston Telegraph,* July 6, 1876; "Minute Book, HE&WT Ry., December 4, 1877," Southern Pacific Papers.

[8]"Journal No. 1, HE&WT Ry, November 7, 18, 1876," 18, 31, 110, Southern Pacific Papers; Reed, *Texas Railroads,* 68. Burton worked for the HE&WT as master mechanic and shop supervisor until his death in 1886.

[9]*Houston Telegraph,* April 18, 1878. November 16, 1878; "Journal No. 1, HE&WT Ry., May 8, 1878," 122; "Minute Book, HE&WT Ry., December 3, 1878," Southern Pacific Papers.

[10]*Houston Telegraph,* April 20, 1878. The name of the Houston paper varies from *Telegraph* to *Telegram* and back again. Sometimes the word *Daily* is part of the title and sometimes it is not. The author has tried to remain consistent when referring to the same paper.

[11]The village of Shepherd was named for B. A. Shepherd, a Houston banker, land speculator, and stockholder in the HE&WT who laid out the town in 1875 and was largely responsible for the route of the road through this town.

[12]"Corporate History of the HE&WT Ry.," Southern Pacific Papers; *Houston Telegraph,* April 18, 1879*; Nacogdoches News,* July 20, 1877.

[13]*Prospectus of the Houston East and West Texas Railway* (New York, 1880), Southern Pacific Papers. This rare pamphlet, signed by Paul Bremond and Samuel Timpson, also discussed the financial structure of the road and its outstanding indebtedness. The map is invaluable in tracing the proposed route of the mainline.

[14]*Houston Telegraph,* July 6, 1876.

[15]*Nacogdoches News,* July 20, 1877; *Burke's Almanac, 1879,* 108; "Minute Book, HE&WT Ry., March 8, and December 5, 1876," Southern Pacific Papers. The records give no indication of reasons but it is quite possible that the order of cause and effect was reversed; i.e., the other business leaders of Houston might have declined to invest heavily in the enterprise primarily because Bremond appeared determined to dominate the company and to dictate its decisions.

[16]"Journal No. 1, HE&WT Ry., 1876–1882," 5, 114, 299; "Ledger No. 2 (1881–1882), HE&WT Ry., 10–11, Southern Pacific Papers.

[17]Nacogdoches County Records; Deeds, Vols. V. 151, W. 254, and W. 229, County Clerk's Office, Nacogdoches, Texas; Harris County Records; Deeds, Vol. 27, 165–175, County Clerk's Office, Houston, Texas. It is a family tradition that the Bremond family suffered because of the casual intermingling of funds. His widow and children lost substantial property because of this confusion. From a conversation with Mrs. Edith Bremond Koch, October 30, 1958, Houston, Texas.

[18]*Houston Telegraph,* December 7, 1876.

[19]*Nacogdoches News,* July 20, 1877. The central committee included such names as Dr. J. H. McCardell, Dr. J. J. Cannon, T. F. Meece, J. P. Kale, and J. E. Hill. For a time Livingston was the northern terminal of the road.

[20]*Houston Telegraph,* November 23, 1878.

[21]From conversations with T. E. Baker, F. I. Tucker, J. Roy Gray, all of Nacogdoches.

[22]"Minute Book, HE&WT Ry., July 3, 1877, December 4, 1877," Southern Pacific Papers; Nacogdoches County Records, Deeds, W-224; Harris County Records, Mortgages, Vol. 8, 167; Henry V. Poor, *Manual of the Railroads of the United States, 1885* (New York, 1886), 825; "Ledger No. 2, HE&WT Ry.," 274–75, Southern Pacific Papers.

[23]"Minute Book, HE&WT Ry., December 7, 1880," Southern Pacific Papers.

[24]*Houston Telegraph,* April 18, 1879; *Nacogdoches News.* July 20, 1877; "Corporate History of the HE&WT Ry.," Southern Pacific Papers; *Burke's Almanac, 1881* (Dallas, 1881), 96.

[25]*Burke's Almanac, 1879* (Dallas, 1879). 100; *1880,* 119; *Houston Post,* October 8, 17, November 2, 7, 1880. The Western Narrow Gauge Railroad became the Texas Western Narrow Gauge and then the Texas Western Railway. But it was eventually abandoned without experiencing any considerable success or profit. Reed, *Texas Railroads,* 478, 540–42.

[26]"Corporate History of the HE&WT Ry.," Southern Pacific Papers; Walter P. Webb. ed., *Handbook of Texas* (2 vols., Austin, 1952), II, 92; *Houston Post,* October 22, 1880.

[27]Angelina County Deeds, K-335, K-338, T-339; *Lufkin Daily News*, October 30, 1955; Webb, ed., *Handbook of Texas*, II, 92. Later Howe was added on the north edge of the central section in honor of M. G. Howe, Master Commissioner and Receiver for the road after 1885.

[28]Webb, ed., *Handbook of Texas,* 11, 92; *Lufkin Daily News,* October 30, 1955,

[29]"Corporate History of the HE&WT Ry.," in the Southern Pacific Papers; Angelina County Deeds, passim; *Prospectus* of the HE&WT Ry.; Nacogdoches County Deeds, V-151, W-254; conversation with Mr. H. L. Bell, Assistant General Manager, Southern Pacific Lines, Houston, March 23, 1955.

[30]*Burke's Texas Almanac,* 1881 (Houston, 1881), 67.

[31]Taylor, "Through Texas," 706; *Burke's Texas Almanac, 1881, 67*; *Nacogdoches News,* July 20, 1877; March 16, 1882.

[32]*Houston Post,* February 22, 1883. Freight service between Houston and Lewisville had been inaugurated November 30, 1882. No mention was made of sidings or a turnaround, but it is assumed that both were constructed. See also *Burke's Texas Almanac, 1883*, 165.

[33]This story, with minor variations, has been recounted to the author by a number of older citizens from Nacogdoches who vouched for its accuracy in its essential details. This helps account for the otherwise unexplainable delay of the railroad in reaching Nacogdoches. From conversations with T. E. Baker, J. F. Summers, F. I. Tucker, Wm. Slay, J. N. Davidson, and J. Roy Gray, all of Nacogdoches.

[34]Nacogdoches County Records, County Clerks Office, Nacogdoches: Deeds, F. H. Hoya to HE&WT, W-243-244; Emily S. Wells to HE&WT, W-244; J. J. Hayter to HE&WT, W-247; W. P. Mimms to HE&WT, W-521; J. P. Davidson to HE&WT, W-252.

[35]*Houston Post,* May 25, 1883; "Corporate History of HE&WT Ry.," Southern Pacific Papers.

[36] *Burke's Texas Almanac, 1885* (Houston, 1885), 53.

III. Completion and Receivership

[1]"Corporate History of HE&WT Ry.," L. A. Loggins to J. C. Carter, February 18, 1952, Southern Pacific Papers; *Nacogdoches News,* October 16, 1884; Webb, ed., *Handbook of Texas,* I, 56.

[2]Nacogdoches County Records, Deeds W-529–532, W-224; "Minute Book, HE&WT Ry., December 5, 1893, May 31, 1884, August 15, 1885, December 4, 1884," Southern Pacific Papers; *Nacogdoches News,* October 16, 1884.

[3]*Poor's Manual of Railroads, 1885,* 825.

[4]Gammel, ed., *Laws of Texas,* 1876 VIII, 989–90; Reed, *Texas Railroads,* 154.

[5]Gammel, ed., *Laws of Texas,* 1882, IX, 263; Volney E. Ramsey, "A History of Land Grants to Texas Railroads," (master's thesis, North Texas State College, 1949).

[6]*Abstract of All Original Texas Land Titles,* General Land Office (Austin, 1941, 8 vols.), passim.

[7]Ibid., vols. III and VII; the earliest certificates were patented by the HE&WT itself in Crockett and Sutton counties. There is one exception, a private entry listed as being filed in Gillespie in December, 1878.

[8]"Minute Book, HE&WT Ry., May 15, 1882," Southern Pacific Papers; Charles B. Leggott, General Land Office, to author, October 11, 1957, December 12, 1957; Reed, *Texas Railroads,* 171. Reed says that since the land was located in the Panhandle the company did not wish to retain title to the land and the entire acreage was sold for $90,970. This statement however, cannot be reconciled with the records of the General Land Office.

[9]"Minute Book, HE&WT Ry., May 15, 1882," Southern Pacific Papers. It is certain, of course, that the scrip brought considerably less than the lands already patented and it could well be that Reed's figure of $90,970 represented the entire return from the land grant.

[10]*Laborer's Champion* (Center, Texas), November 29, 1877; *Texas Almanac, 1871,* (Galveston, 1871), 149; *Burke's Texas Almanac, 1881,* (Houston, 1881), 128; "Corporate History of HE&WT RY.," Southern Pacific Papers.

[11]"Corporate History of the Houston and Shreveport Railroad Company," Southern Pacific Papers; *Nacogdoches News,* October 16, 1884; *Dallas Morning News,* October 1, 1885.

[12]"Minute Book," Board of Directors Meeting, May 17, 1884; "Corporate History of HE&WT Ry.," Southern Pacific Papers. *Nacogdoches News,* July 23, 1885; *Handbook of Texas,* I, 723, 781. The village of Paxton was also established in 1885, as a station on the railroad. It was named for a local pioneer family.

[13]*Houston Post,* May 9, 1885.

[14]*Houston Post.* May 9, 1885. The several inaccuracies in the above account may be explained by the fact that this account appeared in the same paper that carried the Galveston dispatch. No doubt the city editor simply wrote what he recalled of Bremond's career at the moment with no references or records at hand to check his statements.

[15]"Editorial," *Houston Post,* May 12, 1883.

[16]"Plat Map," Glenwood Cemetery, Houston, Texas; quoted from the *San Antonio Express,* in the *Houston Post, May* 16, 1885.

[17]"Minute Book, Stockholders and Board of Directors, HE&WT Ry., June 26, 1885; July 4, 1885; December 1, 1885; December 8, 1885;" Southern Pacific Papers. T. W. House had served as treasurer since 1884. He and Crosby had been directors since that date.

[18]The King Bridge Company "completed and delivered" the bridge to the HE&WT on January 28, 1886. For the structure the company was paid $14,500. "HE&WT Ry., Ledger 2, January 28, 1886, April 22, 1886," Southern Pacific Papers. S. G. Reed gives the date of completion of the bridge across the Sabine and the first through train as January, 1889. This is obviously an error, perhaps merely a typographical error. But the 1889 date has been widely copied by secondary writers, some connected with the Southern Pacific system itself. See Reed, *Texas Railroads*, 237.

IV. Financial Structure, Organization, and Operations

[1]Volney E. Ramsey, "A History of Land Grants to Texas Railroads" (master's thesis, North Texas State College, 1949), 60; *Texas Almanac*, 1958–1959 (Dallas, 1959), 190.

[2]*Houston Telegraph*, April 18, 1878.

[3]*Houston Post*, October 8, 1880; October 17, 1880.

[4]*Houston Post*, November 2, 1880; November 7, 1880; Webb, ed., *Handbook of Texas*, I, 248.

[5]"HE&WT, Journal no. 1, 1876–1882," 114–121, Southern Pacific Papers. Expenditures were also modest—an item in the same Journal records payment "for running engine" $76.05, and for "fireman" $43.50. Both items were for one month's wages. Ibid., 67.

[6]Ibid., 136–158. An item on July 31, 1878 listed $256.25 for "fares received from picnics."

[7]"HE&WT, Ledger, 1881–1882," 167–186, Southern Pacific Papers.

[8]"HE&WT, Journal no. 1, 1876–1882," 164–188ff. The interior stations listed in 1882 were: Cleveland, Shepherd, Goodrich, Livingston, Moscow, Neches, Lufkin, and Lewisville. The total income from these stations in 1882 appears to have been less than $75,000.

[9]Henry V. Poor, *Manual of the Railroads of the United States, 1883,* (New York, 1884), 868; Ibid., *1885*, 825; Ibid., *1887,* 746–47.

[10]"Journal no. 4, HE&WT, 1885;" "Ledger, HE&WT, 1885–1889," 247ff., Southern Pacific Papers.

[11]John F. Stover, *The Railroads of the South, 1865–1900* (Chapel Hill, N.C.), 130–34. Stover also found that most of the roads headed for receivership had a large proportion of northern directors. Prior to Bremond's death only Wil-

liam Marsh Rice was listed as being from New York among the HE&WT directors. Poor, *Manual of Railroads, 1887*, 746–47.

[12]HE&WT Ry. et al *vs.* Jacob Bing et al, Harris County Records vol. Annex T-4, 216; "Ledger, HE&WT, 1893," 303; "Minute Book" HE&WT February 28, 1893; "Corporate History of Houston and Shreveport Railroad Company;" Houston and Shreveport Railroad Charter, Southern Pacific Papers. It was at this time that the name of the Louisiana segment of the road was changed to Houston and Shreveport from Shreveport and Houston.

[13]"Journal no. 4, HE&WT, 1885–1889;" "Ledger, HE&WT, 1893–1897," Southern Pacific Papers.

[14]*Houston Telegraph*, April 20, 1878; April 24, 1878; April 26, 1878.

[15]Ibid., May 21, 1878.

[16]Ibid., November 16, 1878.

[17]*Houston* Post, February 22, 1883.

[18]*Nacogdoches News,* October 16, 1884; July 23, 1885; February 22, 1885.

[19]*The Star News* (Nacogdoches), May 13, 1887.

[20]*Nacogdoches Chronicle*, June 15, 1892. Similar advertisements announced the same schedule in the *Nacogdoches News,* May 13, 1887; and the *Nacogdoches Star News,* March 9, 1888.

[21]*Nacogdoches Star News,* July 22, 1892.

[22]*Nacogdoches Chronicle,* November 18, 1897. See also *Nacogdoches Daily Sentinel*, June 24, 1909.

[23]*Star News* (Nacogdoches, Texas), May 31, 1889.

V. Reorganization and Consolidation

[1]"HE&WT Journal," vol. 50; "Corporate History of HE&WT," Southern Pacific Papers; Angelina County Records, Deeds, U-172. Second mortgage bonds at six percent had been pledged to secure the loan of Paul Bremond, and some 73,800 acres of land in East Texas was sold for $100,000, evidently to satisfy this claim; *Poor's Manual of Railroads, 1893*, 303.

[2]*Dallas Morning News*, February 8, 1896; Joseph B. Polley, *Hood's Texas Brigade* (New York, 1910), 309, 114, 299; "Ledger no. 2, HE&WT, 1881–1882," 10–11, Southern Pacific Papers.

[3]"Minute Book, May 21, 1894," Southern Pacific Papers; "Great Day on the Rabbit," *Southern Pacific Bulletin* (Houston, Texas), September, 1957. S.G. Reed in his *History of Texas Railroads* says that in 1894 the HE&WT was acquired by "Blair and Company, Bankers of New York" who placed it in charge of Norman S. Meldrum as president. The company records do not indicate such a transaction but list James H. Blair as a director of the HE&WT

and H&S and Meldrum as general manager of both roads. See Reed, *Texas Railroads*, 237.

[4]"Recollections of Maurice Brown Harrington" (formerly accountant for T&NO), in "Great Day on the Rabbit," 22; interview with W. F. Rentzel (one time engineer on Southern Pacific Lines), March 29, 1955, Nacogdoches, Texas; "HE&WT Ledger, 1893–1897," Southern Pacific Papers.

[5]"HE&WT Journal," vol. 50, December 7, 1897, Southern Pacific Papers.

[6]In his manuscript history of the Southern Pacific Lines, H. M. Mayo says that "the entire property of the HE&WT and the H&S came under the control of the Southern Pacific Lines in 1893." The present writer is of the opinion that this is in error, perhaps because of a misreading by Mayo of the corporate history of the road. The company records give no indication of a take-over by the Southern Pacific Lines prior to 1899. See H. M. Mayo, "History of the Southern Pacific Lines;" "Corporate History of the HE&WT Ry.," Southern Pacific Papers.

[7]"HE&WT Stockholders Meeting, December 7, 1897," Southern Pacific Papers; *Poor's Manual of Railroads, 1897,* 193; *Poor's Manual of Railroads, 1899*, 545. Jemison had received a quantity of first mortgage bonds and in turn assumed the obligation to change the gauge. His widow had to gain recognition that the contract had been fulfilled before she was released. "HE&WT Director's Meeting, December 1, 1896," Southern Pacific Papers.

[8]"Corporate History of the H&S RR," "H&S Ledger, 1891–1894;" "Minute Book, H&S RR, October 23, 1891," Southern Pacific Papers.

[9]"Contract between HE&WT and H&S RR, July 1, 1897, and December 7, 1897; and "Contract between HE&WT and H&S and Western Union Telegraph Co., April 19, 1898." HE&WT vol. 50; Southern Pacific Papers; Gammel, ed., *Laws of Texas*, 26th Legislature, ch. 73, 110.

[10]*Poor's Manual of Railroads, 1900,* 480; "HE&WT Ledger, 1879–1902," Southern Pacific Papers.

[11]"HE&WT Minute Book, December 5, 1899; December 3, 1901;" John Lansdale to W. E. Oxsheer, December 30, 1930, Southern Pacific Papers; *Poor's Manual of Railroads, 1901,* 642–43; Reed, *Texas Railroads,* 422.

[12]"HE&WT," vol. 50, Southern Pacific Papers; conversation with W. F. Rentzel, March 29, 1955.

[13]"Interstate Commerce Commission Rulings, Docket no. 3918" (March 11, 1912), quoted in Reed, *Texas Railroads,* 627.

[14]"Commissary Records, Angelina County Lumber Company," Kurth Papers, Stephen F. Austin State University Library; *Nacogdoches Chronicle,* January 13, 1894.

[15]*Houston, East & West Texas Railway Company* v. *The United States*, 234 U.S. 342 (1914). The Texas and Pacific Railroad was also a party to the suit. The Commission cited the rate on wagons from Dallas to Marshall, 148 miles, was 36.8¢, but the rate on the same item from Shreveport to Marshall, forty-two miles, was 56¢.

[16]"Commissary Records, Angelina County Lumber Company," Kurth Papers.

[17]Reed, *Texas Railroads*, 626.

[18]Carl B. Swisher, *American Constitutional Development* (New York, 1954), 541; Reed, *Texas Railroads*, 627.

[19]Swisher, *American Constitutional Development*, 541.

[20]*Houston, East & West Texas Railway Company* v. *United States*, 234 U.S. 342; Merlo J. Pusey, *Charles Evans Hughes* (2 vols. New York, 1951), 1:307–08.

[21]Swisher, *American Constitutional Development*, 541–43; Reed, *Texas Railroads*, 629–40.

[22]"Corporate History of the HE&WT;" Lansdale to Oxsheer, December 30, 1930; Southern Pacific Papers; Neill C. Wilson and Frank J. Taylor, *Southern Pacific, The Roaring Story of* a *Fighting Railroad* (New York, 1952), 155.

VI. Connecting Lines

[1]Reed, *Texas Railroads*, passim.

[2]Lawrence L. Waters, *Steel Trails to Santa Fe* (Lawrence, Kansas, 1950), 76–79, 346–47; Reed, *Texas Railroads*, 292–94.

[3]Waters, *Steel Trails to Santa Fe*, 347; John O. King, *The Early History of The Houston Oil Company of Texas* (Houston, 1959), 7, passim; Reed, Texas Railroads, 293; *The Kirby Story*, The Kirby Lumber Company (Houston, 1951). The Santa Fe repeatedly loaned Kirby funds to expand his operations, taking stocks and bonds of the Kirby companies as security. Eventually, after the death of Kirby, the Kirby Lumber Company became a Santa Fe subsidiary.

[4]Benjamin A. Botkin and Alvin F. Harlow, *A Treasury of Railroad Folklore* (New York, 1953), 285, 506.

[5]Reed, *Texas Railroads*, 484; Vincent V. Masterson, *The Katy Railroad and the Last Frontier* (Norman, Okla., 1952), 280.

[6]Conversation with T. L. Epperson, Trinity, June 5, 1962; Lucius Beebe, *Mixed Train Daily* (New York, 1947), 96, 111, 318, 332; Masterson, *The Katy Railroad*, 282–84; Reed, *Texas Railroads*, 284–87; *Houston Chronicle*, April 22, 1962.

[7]Reed, *Texas Railroads*, 457.

[8]Botkin, *A Treasury of Railroad Folklore*, 242; Joe R. Thompson, "Steaming in the Rain," *Trains*, August, 1960, 26–27; Reed, *Texas Railroads*, 461; *Dallas Morning News*, May 20, October 22, 1956, March 17, 1962; Beebe, *Mixed Train Daily*, 111.

[9]Masterson, *The Katy Railroad*, 227. James Stanley Joyce, a Chicago lumber millionaire, was known chiefly as the one-time husband of stage and film star Peggy Hopkins Joyce. The Thompson family had a number of large mills in East Texas, including plants at Trinity, Kilgore, Grayburg, and Doucette.

[10]Masterson, *The Katy Railroad*, 227.

[11]Ibid., 227, 235, 282–84; Reed, *Texas Railroads*, 284–86.

[12]*Lufkin Daily News*, October 30, 1955; Reed, *Texas Railroads*, 477.

[13]Reed, *Texas Railroads*, 477–78; *Houston Post*, January 28, February 4, 1962.

[14]*Texas Almanac, 1958–1959*, (Dallas, 1959), 276. *New Birmingham, Texas* (New Birmingham, Texas 1891), pamphlet in East Texas Collections, Stephen F. Austin State University Library. *New Birmingham Times*, February 23, 1889.

[15]*Star News* (Nacogdoches), May 31, 1889; May 22, 1891; *Daily Phone* (Nacogdoches), August 8, 1899. Note: The St. Louis, Arkansas & Texas Ry. acquired control of the Texas and St. Louis Railway in 1886.

[16]*The Daily Phone* (Nacogdoches), August 8, 1899.

[17]Reed, *Texas Railroads*, 418–21.

[18]Conversation with W. S. Scott, Gen. Mgr. A&NR, Keltys, Texas, June 6, 1962; Beebe, *Mixed Train Daily*, 111, 331, 338; Reed, *Texas Railroads*, 443; interview with N. J. Terry, Keltys, Texas, July 29, 1958. More recently (1957) the T&NO abandoned its sixteen miles of track between Dunagan and Nacogdoches and uses the A&NR tracks to connect with the HE&WT north of Lufkin. (W. S. Scott to author, September 21, 1962.)

[19]Conversations with Ernest L. Kurth, Sr., Keltys, Texas, 1955–1958; Frank W. Johnson, *A History of Texas and Texans* (New York, 1914), V, 3483. Other members of the parent corporation active in the management of the A&NR included Eli Wiener who served as president of the railroad for many years.

[20]Records of the Angelina and Neches River Railroad, in the Kurth Papers, Stephen F. Austin State University. Conversation with W. S. Scott, General Mgr. A&NR RR., June 6, 1962.

[21]Reed, *Texas Railroads*, 230–31; conversation with Thomas E. Baker, 1954. *The Daily Phone* (Nacogdoches), July 26, August 8, 1899.

[22]Reed, *Texas Railroads*, 232.

[23]"Corporate History of the T&NO," Southern Pacific Papers.

[24]*The Houston Post*. September 9, 1957; *The Daily Phone* (Nacogdoches). August 8, 1899; Reed, *Texas Railroads,* 233.

[25]*Texas Almanac, 1961–1962* (Dallas, 1962), 143; Rupert N. Richardson, *Texas, the Lone Star State* (Englewood Cliffs, NJ, 1958), 344.

[26]"Minute Book," Nacogdoches and Southeastern Railroad, 1905–1926, in the Stephen F. Austin State University Library, Nacogdoches, Texas.

[27]*Tyler Morning Telegraph*, Thursday, January 13, 1949.

[28]Ibid.; Reed, *Texas Railroads,* 461–62.

[29]Reed, *Texas Railroads*, 479–80.

[30]A Mr. F. T. Rembert and associates quietly bought up these independent short lines as they became available. Evidently he acquired them for the Santa Fe but that did not become apparent until 1904. Reed, *Texas Railroads,* 294–95.

[31]Waters, *Steel Trails to Santa Fe*, 347, 363; Reed, *Texas Railroads*, 295. Evidently the Santa Fe had planned to build the connecting line by way of Grigsby but later decided on the route through Center. When the timber was cut out the Grigsby branch was abandoned.

[32]Arthur E. Stilwell and James R. Crowell, "I had a Hunch," *The Saturday Evening Post,* January 14, 1928, 77–78.

VII. "The Rabbit"

[1]Botkin, *A Treasury of Railroad Folklore*, 506.

[2]*Houston Post,* September 9, 1957.

[3]Conversation with T. E. Baker, Nacogdoches, Texas, 1954; and Mrs. Carolyn Sturdevant Miller, Nacogdoches, 1962.

[4]*Dallas Morning News*, March 13, 1962. Bobo today is called Meldrum (for N. S. Meldrum), and Blair is called Gallagher. See *The Lufkin News*, Sunday, July 15, 1962.

[5]From Tex Ritter, "Tenaha, Timpson, Bobo and Blair," Capital Records, (15375). Courtesy Dr. Karl Schlicher, T. F. Essery, and Mrs. Mozelle Winfree, One version calls it the H&TC Line.

Bibliography

PRIMARY SOURCES

Manuscripts

East Texas Papers: Bennett Blake Papers; Miscellaneous Collection, Stephen F. Austin State University Library.

Southern Pacific Papers. This collection includes the *Prospectus*; Contract between HE&WT and H&S RR.; Contract between HE&WT and H&S and Western Union Telegraph Company; "Corporate History of HE&WT Ry.;" "Corporate History of Houston and Shreveport Railroad Company;" L. A. Loggins to J. C. Carter, February 18, 1952; HE&WT Journals vols. 1, 2, 4, 50; HE&WT Ledgers 1 & 2; "Minute Book." John Lansdale to W. E. Oxheer, December 30, 1930; and "Mayo Manuscript" on History of Southern Pacific Lines. All are in the Regional Office, Houston, Texas.

Kemp, Louis, Sketch of Paul Bremond, n.d., (manuscript in possession of Mrs. Edith Bremond Koch, Houston, Texas).

Kurth Papers. Commissary Records, Angelina County Lumber Company, in the Stephen F. Austin State College Library.

Interviews

Conversation with Thomas E. Baker, Nacogdoches, Texas, 1954.

Conversation with H. L. Bell, Assistant General Manager, Southern Pacific Lines, Houston, Texas, March 23, 1955.

Conversation with T. L. Epperson, Trinity, Texas, June 5, 1962.

Conversations with Ernest L. Kurth, Sr., Keltys, Texas, 1955–1958.

Conversation with Mrs. Carolyn Sturdevant Miller, Nacogdoches, Texas, 1962.

Conversations with J. F. Summers, T. E. Baker, F. I. Tucker, William Slay, J. N. Davidson, and J. Roy Gray, all of Nacogdoches, 1955–1962.

Conversation with W. S. Scott, General Manager A&NR, Keltys, Texas, June 6, 1962.

Conversation with Mrs. Edith B. Koch, October 30, 1958, Houston, Texas.
Conversation with W. F. Rentzel, March 29, 1955, Nacogdoches, Texas.
Conversation with N. J. Terry, Keltys, Texas, July 29, 1958.

Printed Sources: Government Publications and Records

Abstract of All Original Texas Land Titles, General Land Office, 8 vols., Austin, 1941.

Angelina County Deeds: K-335, K-338, T-339, County Clerk's Office, Lufkin, Texas.

Gammel, H. P. N., ed. *The Laws of Texas,* 10 vols., Austin, 1898.

Harris County Records: Deeds, vol. 27, County Clerk's Office, Houston, Texas.

Harris County Records: Mortgages, vol. 8, County Clerk's Office, Houston, Texas.

Houston, East & West Texas Railway Company v *The United States,* 234 U.S. 342 (1914).

Nacogdoches County Records: Deeds, County Clerk's Office, Nacogdoches, Texas.

"Plat Map," Glenwood Cemetery, Houston, Texas.

SECONDARY WORKS

Books

Association of American Railroads. *American Railroads, Their Growth and Development* (Washington, 1954).

Beebe, Lucius. *Mixed Train Daily* (New York, 1947).

Botkin, Benjamin A. and Harlow, Alvin F. *Treasury of Railroad Folklore* (New York, 1953).

Burke's Texas Almanac (Houston, 1879, 1880, 1881, 1883, 1885).

Carroll, H. Bailey. *Standard History of Houston* (Knoxville, Tennessee, 1912).

Hanford, Albert, ed. *Texas State Register and Almanac* (Houston, 1876).

Johnson, Frank W. *A History of Texas and Texans* (5 vols., New York, 1914).

King, John O. *The Early History of the Houston Oil Company of Texas* (Houston, 1959).

Masterson, Vincent V. *The Katy Railroad and the Last Frontier* (Norman, Okla., 1952).

Poor, Henry V. *Manual of the Railroads of the United States.* (New York, 1883–1901).

Pusey, Merlo J. *Charles Evans Hughes* (2 vols. New York, 1951).
Reed, St. Clair G. *A History of the Texas Railroads* (Houston, 1941),
Richardson, Rupert N. *Texas, The Lone Star State* (Englewood Cliffs, NJ, 1958).
Stover, John F. *The Railroads of the South,* 1865–1900 (Chapel Hill, 1955).
Swisher, Carl B. *American Constitutional Development* (New York, 1954).
Taylor, Frank J. and Wilson, Neill C. *Southern Pacific, The Roaring Story of a Fighting Railroad* (New York, 1955).
Taylor, George Rogers and Neu, Irene D. *The American Railroad Network,* 1861–1890 (Cambridge, MA, 1956).
Texas Almanac. Published by *Dallas Morning News* (Dallas, 1959).
Waters, Lawrence L. *Steel Trails to Santa Fe* (Lawrence, KS, 1950).
Webb, Walter Prescott, ed. *Handbook of Texas* (2 vols., Austin, 1952).
Young, Dr. S. O. *Thumb-Nail History of Houston* (Houston, 1912).

Periodicals

Stilwell, Arthur E. and James R. Crowell, "I Had a Hunch," *The Saturday Evening Post,* January 14, 1928.
Taylor, Frank H., "Through Texas," *Harper's Monthly,* 59:706 (1879).
Thompson, Joe R., "Steaming in the Rain," in *Trains,* August, 1960.

Pamphlets and Bulletins

"Great Day on the Rabbit." *Southern Pacific Bulletin*, Houston, September, 1957.

Newspapers

Daily Phone (Nacogdoches, Texas), July 26, 1899; August 8, 1899.
Dallas Morning News (Dallas, Texas), October 1, 1885; January 26, 31, 1886; May 20, 1956; October 22, 1956; March 17, 1962.
Houston Chronicle (Houston, Texas), April 22, 1962.
Houston Post (Houston, Texas), November 16, 1878; October 8, 17, 22, 1880; November 2, 7, 1880; February 22, 1883; May 25, 1883; May 9, 1885; January 26, 27, 30, 1886; September 9, 1957.
Houston Evening Post (Houston, Texas), February 20, 1880.
Houston Telegraph (Houston, Texas), July 6, 1876; December 8, 1876; April 18, 1878; April 20, 1878; November 23, 1878; April 18, 1879.
Laborer's Champion (Center, Texas), November 29, 1877.
Lufkin Daily News (Lufkin, Texas), October 30,1955.

Nacogdoches Chronicle (Nacogdoches, Texas), June 15, 1892; November 18, 1897.
Nacogdoches News (Nacogdoches, Texas), July 20, 1877; March 17, 1882; October 17, 1884; February 22, 1885; July 23, 1885; January 30, 1886; March 13, 1887.
Nacogdoches Sentinel (Nacogdoches, Texas), 1900–1909.
Star News (Nacogdoches, Texas), July 22, 1892; May 13, 1887; March 9, 1888; May 31, 1889; May 22, 1891.
Tyler Morning Telegraph (Tyler, Texas), Jan. 13, 1949.

Records

Capital Records, (15375), by Tex Ritter, "Tenaha, Timpson, Bobo and Blair."

Index

Abstract of Texas Land Titles, 29
Adams, C. M., 45
Africa, Texas, 15, 46
African-Americans. (*See* Negroes.)
Alexander, A. C., 45
Alexander, R. J., 45
Allen, Ebenezer, 7
Allen, Sam, 60
Anderson County, 61
Anderson, T. J., 44, 51
Angelina and Neches River Railroad, 85, 86, 90, 112n
Angelina County, 18, 22, 23, 80
Angelina County Lumber Company, 85, 86, 87 (photo)
Angelina River, 18, 23, 24, 62, 76, 84, 85, 90, 96, 102
Appleby, Harriet. (*See* Harriet Bremond.)
Appleby, James, 8, 27, 37, 43, 60
Appleby, Texas, 27, 45, 46, 101
Atchison, Topeka and Santa Fe Railroad, 72, 73, 94
Attoyac Bayou, 31
Attoyac River, 27, 85, 89, 90
Auburn, Texas, 75
Austin, Texas, 4

Baker, James A., Jr., 60
Baker, Moseley, 9, 36, 102
Baldwin locomotives, 62
Bandera County, 30
Banita Creek, 27
Banita Junction, Texas, 88
Barnum, Texas, 76
Battle of San Jacinto, 9
Beaumont and Great Northern Railway, 73–75
Beaumont, Sour Lake and Western, 72
Beaumont, Texas, 4, 5, 72, 74, 87, 88, 92, 103n
Big Sandy, Texas, 82
Big Thicket, Texas, 77
Blair, James H., 109n
Blair, Texas, 46, 98, 101, 113n
Blanchard, Texas, 73
Blix, Texas, 81
Bobo, Texas, 46, 98, 113n
Botts, Ben A., 13
Brady, J. T., 13
Brashear, Henry, 60
Brazos Plank Road, 6, 7
Brazos Valley, 6
Bremond, Catherine Green. (*See* Catherine Green.)
Bremond, Edward L., 8, 19, 31, 37, 44, 48, 63
Bremond, Harriet, 8
Bremond, Harriet Martha Sprouls. (*See* Harriet Martha Sprouls.)
Bremond, Julia, 9
Bremond, Kate, 9, 18
Bremond, Margaret, 8

Bremond, Mary E. Van Alstyne. (*See* Mary E. Van Alstyne.)
Bremond, Mary Louise. (*See* Viscountess de Valernes.)
Bremond, Nettie, 9
Bremond, Paul, early life, 5; hat making, 5, 6; to Texas, 6; Houston businessman, 6; interest in railroads, 6; builds H&TC, 1, 6–7; relations with employees, 7, 8; family, 8; spiritualist, 9; appearance, 9–10; organizes HE&WT, 11–13; builds road, 13–26; urges local support for railway, 13, 17; finances railway, 17, 27–28; secures land grant, 12, 15, 28; dies, 32; eulogies, 32, 32–33, 33–35; as president, 46
Bremond, Paul Barlie, 5
Bremond, Pauline, 9
Bremond's Road, 17, 18, 21, 24, 31, 41, 46, 62, 64, 65, 66, 67, 69, 71, 76, 80, 88, 92, 93, 94, 101
Brewster County, 30
Bright, L. B., 45
Briscoe, P., 45
broad-gauge railroads, 11, 16, 35, 40
Bryan, E. A., 45
Buena Vista, Texas, 30, 31
Buffalo Bayou, Brazos, and Colorado Railroad, 3
Burke, Ed, 22
Burke, Texas, 22, 40, 45, 46, 51, 101
Burton, Charles A., 14, 104n
Burton, J. E., 45
Butler, Frank N., 63
Bynum, G. M., 45
Calgary, Texas, 89, 90
Camden, Texas, 76
Camino Real (El), 23
Camp Pershing, Texas, 90
Camp Ruby, Texas, 76
Camp Worth, Texas, 90
Cannon, Dr. J. J., 105n
Carlisle, William, 73, 74
Carmona, Texas, 78
Carter, W. T., and Brothers Lumber Company, 76, 77, 96, 101
Carthage, Texas, 92
Cave, E. W., 13
Cedar, Texas. (*See* Gossett, Texas.)
Centennial Exposition,
"Centennial" locomotive, 14
Center, Texas, 92, 113n
Central and Montgomery Railway, 72
Central Texas, 6
Cheeseman, A. W., 45
Chicago, Illinois, 73, 94
Chireno, Texas, 85
Chronister Lumber Company, 82
Cincinnati Bridge Company, 14
Civil War, 1, 3, 5, 61, 87
Clawson Lumber Company, 82
Clayton, A. J., 45
Cleveland, Texas, 14, 15, 45, 46, 47, 51, 72, 92, 96, 101, 108n
Cleveland, W. D., 13
Climax, Texas, 24, 97
Collins, John, 45
Collins, R. S., 38, 44, 49, 50, 52, 84
Colmesneil, Texas, 74, 78
Cone, Horace, 19, 44
Conroe, Texas, 72, 92
Corpus Christi, Texas, 12, 17
Corsicana, Texas, 7

Corrigan, Pat, 21
Corrigan, Texas, 21, 45, 48, 50, 51, 77, 78, 80, 101
cotton, 4, 6, 16, 21, 61, 72
Cotton Belt Railroad, (*See also* St. Louis Southwestern Railway.) 22, 65, 80, 81, 82, 85, 92
cotton gins, 40
Coughlin, S. P., 45
Coyote Special, 94
Crocker, Charles, 2
Crockett County, 29, 107n
Crockett, Texas, 5
Crosby, J. F., 44, 108n
Cypress, Texas, 7

Dallas Morning News, 38
Dallas, Texas, 4, 7, 68, 69, 87, 88, 111n
Dargan, E., 37, 44
Darney, W. H., 44
Davidson, L. P., 45
Dennis, John B., 60
Denver and Rio Grande Railroad, 16
Denver, Colorado, 17, 89
Diboll, J. C., 80
Diboll, Texas, 80, 81, 82
Doherty, William, 44
Donohue, F. M., 45
Dorr Junction, Texas, 88
Doucette, Texas, 112n
Dozier, John A., 9, 22, 43
Dozier, Pauline. (*See* Pauline Bremond.)
Duff, R. C., 74
Dunagan Station, Texas, 85, 88, 112n
Dunn, Thomas C., 60

East Tempe, Texas, 73
East Texas, 4, 5, 16, 22, 35, 36, 39 48, 65, 67, 73, 101, 102
Eastern Texas Railroad Company, 5, 103n
Edwards County, 29
El Paso, Texas, 65, 104n
Episcopalians, 9
Estes, O. R., 96
Estill, J. T., 45
Etoile, Texas, 85
Everett, M., 45
excursions, 15, 46, 83, 96

Faubian, J. L., 45
Fernandez, Julie. (*See* Julie Bremond.)
Fernandez, Lucas, 9
Fiquet, D. D., 44
Fishkill, New York, 5
Fitze, Charles G., 27, 44, 48
Fitze, Texas, 27, 46, 101
Floeck, Peter, 13
Ford "railbus," 75
Forey, H. R., 45
Fort Worth and Denver City (Burlington), 71
Fouts Mill, Texas, 21
Fox, Henry, 13
Franks, Louisiana, 46
Frost-Johnson Lumber Company, 89–90, 101
Frost Lumber Industries, 89

Gallagher, Texas, 113n
Galveston and Red River Railroad, 3, 5, 6, 7
Galveston, Harrisburg and San Antonio Railway, 4, 69, 71
Galveston, Houston, and Henderson Railroad, 3, 4, 5, 71

Galveston, Sabine and St. Louis Railway, 91
Galveston, Texas, 3, 4, 6, 14, 17, 32, 35, 61
Garrison, Texas, 27, 45, 46, 50, 51, 67
Gary, Texas, 92
General Land Office of Texas, 29, 107n
Gentry, A. M., 45
Gillespie County, 107n
"Girard," locomotive, 14
Goodrich, Texas, 15, 23, 45, 46, 101, 108n
Goodwin, Major, 15
Gossett, Texas, 88
Gould, Jay, 2, 77, 78, 94
Gray, E. F., 14
Grayburg, Texas, 112n
Great Northern Railroad, 2
Green, Catherine, 5
Green, David Griggs, 76
Greenville, Texas, 76
Grigsby, Texas, 92, 113n
Groce, T. J., 60
Groesbeck, Abraham, 7, 13, 17, 22, 43
Groveton, Lufkin and Northern Railroad, 81
Groveton, Texas, 78
Gulf, Beaumont and Kansas City, 72
Gulf Coast, 4, 14, 37, 73, 74, 89, 93
Gulf, Colorado and Santa Fe, 71, 72, 83
Gulf, Shreveport and Kansas City Railroad Company, 31

Hacknew, Texas, 46
Hardin County, 18
Harris County, 18
Harrisburg, Texas, 3
Hawley, Marcus C., 43, 63
Haynes, B. F., 45
Hayward, E. B., Lumber Company, 89, 101
Heard, D. W., 18
"Hell Either Way Taken," 95
Hemphill, Texas, 75
Hempstead, Texas, 7
Henderson and Burkeville, 5
Henderson and Kurth Lumber Company, 67, 82
Henderson, Texas, 5, 91
Herty, Texas, 85, 86
Hicks family, 32
High Island, Texas, 92
Hill, E. P., 37, 44
Hill, J. E., 105n
Hill, James, J., 2
Homer, Texas, 22, 23
Hood's Brigade, 61
Hopkins County, 18
Hopkins, Mark, 2
House, T. W., 7, 13, 17, 37, 44, 60, 63, 108n
Houston and Shreveport Railroad, 42, 43, 44, 63, 65, 109n
Houston and Texas Central Railway, 3, 4, 7, 11, 13, 49, 69, 71, 83
Houston County, 81
Houston, East and West Texas Railway, history, 1; charter, 11–12; construction, 13–16; *Prospectus*, 16, 23; bonds, 20; by-passes Homer, 23; reaches Nacogdoches, 25; continues construction, 27; second mortgage bonds, 27; receives land grant, 15, 28–29; in

receivership, 37, 60; completion, 37–38; earnings, 41–43, 63, 64–65; equipment, 41–42; financial status, 43; foreclosure and sale, 43, 60; agents, 45; Time Tables, 46–52, 53 (photo); reorganization, 60; made standard gauge, 61–62; and H&S RR, 63–65; in the "Shreveport Case," 66–69
Houston Post, 21, 24, 32, 33, 37, 40
Houston Tap and Brazoria Railway, 3, 103n
Houston Telegraph, 13, 40
Houston, Texas, 3, 4, 5, 6, 7, 8, 9, 13, 14, 15, 17, 19, 23, 24, 25, 30, 32, 33, 35, 36, 37, 38, 43, 45, 46, 47, 48, 49, 50, 61, 65, 66, 67, 68, 69, 71, 72, 77, 83, 84, 87, 92, 96, 97, 98, 106n
"How Easy We Travel," 96
Howe, M. G., 37, 43, 44, 49, 50, 52, 60, 84, 106n
Hughes, Charles Evans, 68–69
Humphrey, C. P., 45
Hunt County, 76
Huntington, Collis P., 2, 87, 88
Hutchins, W. J., 7, 13

International and Great Northern Railroad, 4, 5, 49, 71, 72, 77, 78, 91
Interstate Commerce Commission, 66, 67, 68, 69, 74–75
Irion County, 30
Irish workers, 7, 8

Jacksonville, Texas, 82, 88
Jamerson, J. M., 30
Jasper County, 11, 18
Jemison, E. S., and Company, 18
Jemison, Elbert S., 43, 60, 62, 63, 110n
Jemison, Groce and Company, 61
Jemison, Louise, 62, 110n
Jenkins, J. H., 63
Joaquin, Texas, 32, 45, 46, 47
Johnson, W. P., 45
Jones, J. R., 31
Joyce, James Stanley, 78, 112n
Joyce lumber, 78, 81

Kale, J. P., 105n
Kansas and Gulf Short Line Railroad, 22, 82, 83, 84
Kansas City Southern Railway, 92
Katy. (*See* Missouri, Kansas, Texas Railroad.)
Kaufman, Texas, 88
Keachi, Louisiana, 31, 45, 46, 51
Keith Brothers, 45
Keithville, Louisiana, 45, 46
Keltys, Texas, 85, 86
Kerr County, 29
Kickapoo, Texas, 73
Kilgore, Texas, 112n
King Iron Bridge and Manufacturing Company, 37, 108n
Kirby, John Henry, 72, 73, 92, 111n
Kirby Lumber Company, 111n
Kirbyville, Texas, 92
Knox Lumber Company, 75, 101
Knox, W. H., Sr., 75
Kountze, Texas, 88, 92
Kurth, Ernest L., Jr., 86
Kurth, Ernest L., Sr., 86, 101
Kurth, Joseph H., 86

La Cerda, Texas, 90
Lacy, P. A., 45
land grant to HE&WT, 40, 107n
Laredo, Texas, 12
Leggett, Texas, 46
Lesdenier, L. F. D., 45
Lewisville, Texas, 24, 45, 46, 47, 106n, 108n
Livingston and Southeastern Railroad, 75
Livingston, Texas, 16, 19, 21, 45, 46, 51, 64, 73, 75, 105n, 108n
Logansport, Louisiana, 17, 31, 38, 45, 46, 51, 92
Lombardi, C., 60
Long Island Railroad, 77
Longview and Sabine Valley, 91
Longview, Texas, 4
Looney, J. A., 45
Love Wood Products of Texas, 81
Lovett, R. S., 63
Luce, Texas, 73
Lufkin, Edwin P., 22, 23, 32, 44
Lufkin Foundry, 86
Lufkin Land and Lumber Comapny, 84
Lufkin National Bank, 86
Lufkin, Nettie. (*See* Nettie Bremond.)
Lufkin, Texas, 22, 24, 41, 45, 46, 50, 51, 62, 64, 67, 80, 81, 82, 83, 84, 85, 87, 97, 101, 108n, 112n
Lufkin, Walter, 9, 37
lumbering, 4, 15, 16, 21, 39, 40, 41, 64, 65, 73, 75, 76, 78, 80, 82, 84
Lynn County, 30

Magill, H. A., 45
Marshall, Texas, 16, 103n, 111n
Marshall, Timpson and Sabine Pass Railroad, 92
McCall, D. B., 45
McCardell, Dr. J. H., 105n
Meece, T. F., 105n
Meldrum, Norman S., 60, 63, 109n, 113n
Meldrum, Texas, 101, 113n
Merriman, Texas, 46
Mexican, Henderson and Gulf, 5
Michelli, Vincente, 24
Millegde Station, Texas, 15
Mississippi River, 14
Missouri, Kansas, Texas Railroad, 71, 74, 76, 77, 78
Missouri Pacific Railroad, 2, 72, 78
"Mogul" locomotive, 77
Montgomery County, 14, 18, 72
Montgomery, Texas, 72
Moody, W. S., 61
Moore, A. R., 45
Moore, Francis, 7
Morris, B. F., 32
Morris, Joaquin, 32
Moscow, Camden and San Augustine Railroad, 75
Moscow, Texas, 19, 21, 45, 46, 51, 75, 76, 96, 108n
mule teams, 14, 15, 37, 77

Nacogdoches and Southeastern Railroad, 89–91
Nacogdoches County, 18, 23, 27, 41
Nacogdoches, News (The), 23, 24, 31, 38

Nacogdoches Sentinel, 51
Nacogdoches, Texas, 5, 17, 20, 23, 24, 25, 26, 27, 45, 46, 47, 48, 49, 50, 51, 64, 67, 84, 87, 88, 89, 97, 106n, 112n
narrow-gauge railraods, 10 (photo), 11, 13, 16, 31, 35, 38, 40
Natchez City, 46
Navasota, Texas, 7, 72
Neches River, 4, 21, 22, 81
Neches River bridge, 62
Neches, Texas, 108n
Negroes, 13, 75, 90, 98
New Birmingham, Texas, 82–83
New Caney, Texas, 14, 46, 47
New Orleans, Louisiana, 4, 65
New York Central Lines, 2
New York City, 5, 9, 16, 17, 18, 20, 21, 30, 61, 65, 93
Noble, Frank, 13, 14

O'Connor, J. F., 45
Oil springs, Texas, 89–90
Olin Industries, Inc., 89
Onalaska, Texas, 73
Orange, Texas, 4, 93
oxen teams, 14, 15, 37, 77

Palestine, Texas, 4, 77
Panhandle, 30, 107n
Panic of 1837, 6
Paris, Texas, 92
Parker, Texas, 46
Paxton, Texas, 46, 107n
Peebles, T. M., 45
Pegoda, Texas, 73
Pence, G. W., 45
Perkins, P. M., 45
Philadelphia, Pennsylvania, 6, 11
Philadelphia Centennial Exposition, 11, 14
pig iron, 83
Pillot, Eugene, 13, 17
Piney Woods, The, 4, 5, 10, 13, 16, 19, 21, 26, 30, 35, 36, 38, 39, 41, 72, 77, 78, 85, 87, 88, 90, 91, 101, 102
Polk County, 15, 18, 19, 76
Poor's Manual of Railroads, 41, 42, 43
Port Arthur, Texas, 74, 93
Port Lavaca, 103n
Porter, G. T., 45
Presidio County, 30
puffer belly engines, 14, 94
Pullman coaches, 62
Purviance, W. T., 45

Queen & Crescent Railroad, 49, 50, 83

"Rabbit," 95 (photo)
Ragley-Saner Lumber Company, 91, 101
Railroad Land Grant Law, 29
Real County, 29
Red River, 11, 16, 32
Red River, Sabine and Western Railway, 89
Reklaw, Texas, 88
Rembert, F. T., 113n
Republic of Texas, 3, 6
Rice, F. A., 13, 17
Rice, Margaret. (*See* Margaret Bremond.)
Rice, William Marsh, 6, 7, 8, 37, 108n
Rice University, 8
Richardson, Joseph, 43, 63

Ringling Brothers Circus
excursion, 96
Rio Grande Valley, 30
Ritter, Tex, 99–100
Roberts, J. S., 13
Roberts, W. C., 45
Rock Island Lines, 71–72
Rockland, Texas, 88
Roganville, Texas, 72
Rogers locomotives, 61
Round Prairie, Texas, 15, 46
Rusk County, 91
Rusk, Texas, 82
Rusk Transportation Company, 82
Russell, W. I. F., 45

Sabine and East Texas Railway, 88
Sabine County, 18, 75
Sabine Lake, 93
Sabine Pass, Texas, 5, 75, 88, 103n
Sabine River, 4, 11, 16, 28, 30, 31, 32, 37, 48, 87, 92, 94
Sabine River bridge, 62, 64
Sacul, Texas, 88
San Antonio and Mexican Gulf, 103n
San Antonio Express, 35
San Antonio, Texas, 4, 29, 65
San Augustine, Texas, 24, 76, 92
San Jacinto County, 18, 19
San Jacinto River, 14
San Jacinto River bridge, 14, 15, 62
San Jacinto Springs, 15, 46, 62
San Jacinto, Texas, 46
Santa Fe Railroad, 32, 49, 72–73, 89, 90, 92, 113n
Saron, Texas, 78
Saunders, Texas, 78
sawmills, 15, 16, 40, 68, 72, 81, 82, 89
Schleicher County, 30
Sealy, George, 72
Sears, F. C., 45
Sears, T. S., 45
Seasonburg, Texas, 45
Sebastopol, Texas, 73
Sequoyah, Texas, 73
Shearn, John, 13
Shelby County, 11, 18, 30, 92, 98
Shepherd, B. A., 7, 22, 104n
Shepherd, J. H., 63
Shepherd, Texas, 15, 45, 46, 51, 101, 104n, 108n
Sherman, Texas, 4
short line railroads 1, 2, 3
Shreveport and Houston Railroad, 31, 50, 109n
Shreveport and Red River, 92
Shreveport Case (The), 66–69
Shreveport, Louisiana, 4, 31, 33, 36, 37, 38, 42, 45, 46, 49, 50, 51, 61, 64, 65, 66, 67, 68, 71, 83, 84, 92, 96, 97, 103n, 111n
Silsbee, Texas, 72, 92
Simmons, W. F., 45
Somerville, Texas, 72, 92
Southern Pacific lines, 2, 23, 49, 65, 66, 69, 71, 72, 83, 84, 87, 88, 91, 94, 103n, 110n
Southern Pine Lumber Company, 80, 81
Southland Paper Mills, 85, 86
Spindletop, 93
Spiritual Photography, 9
spiritualism, 9, 33
Sprouls, Harriet Martha, 8
Stafford's Point, Texas, 3
standard-gauge railroads, 61

Stanford, Leland, 2
steam skidders, 85, 86 (photo), 90
Stevens, James H., 7
Stilwell, Arthur E., 92
Stinson, C. D., 44, 45, 49
St. Louis, Arkansas and Texas Railway, 50, 82, 83, 84, 112n
St. Louis, Missouri, 84
St. Louis Southwestern Railway (Cotton Belt), 84, 87
Stoddard, A. B., 45
Stover, John F., 42
Sturdevant, Ira Link, 97–98
Supreme Court of the United States, 68–69
Sutton County, 29, 107n
Sydnor, John, 6

"Tattered, Shattered and Expired," 81
Taylor, Mrs. C. W., 45
Temple Associates, 81
Temple Associates Box Factory, 81
Temple Builders Supply, 81
Temple Industries, 81
Temple Lumber Company, 81
Temple Manufacturing Company, 81
Temple Steel Products Company, 81
Temple, Texas, 78
Temple, Thomas Lewis Latanè, 80–81, 80 (photo), 101
Temple-White Company, 81
Tenaha, Texas, 32, 45, 46, 51, 64, 67, 91, 92, 98
"Tenaha, Timpson, Bobo and Blair," 98, 99
Texarkana, Texas, 4, 11, 17, 80, 93
Texas Alien Land Law, 83
Texas and Gulf, 91
Texas and Louisiana Railroad, 84
Texas and New Orleans Railroad, 3, 4, 5, 13, 65, 69, 71, 78, 84, 85, 87–89, 112n
Texas and Pacific Railway, 4, 16, 49, 50, 82, 83, 92, 111n
Texas and St. Louis Railway of Texas, 82, 112n
Texas Constitution, 28
Texas legislature, 11, 28, 64
Texas, Louisiana & Eastern Railroad, 72
Texas Railroad Commission, 66, 67, 69
Texas Revolution, 9
Texas, Sabine Valley and Northwestern, 91
Texas South-Eastern Railroad, 80, 81
Texas Trunk Railroad, 88
Texas Western Narrow Gauge, 72, 104n, 105n
Texas Western Railway, 105n
Thompson and Tucker Lumber Company, 78, 79 (photo), 101, 112n
"Time No Object," 89
Timpson, Texas, 31, 45, 46, 51, 67, 83, 91, 92, 96, 98, 101
Timpson and Henderson Railway, 91
Timpson, Harriet. (*See* Harriet Bremond.)
Timpson, Paul, 31
Timpson, Samuel Coulter, 8, 13, 31, 43, 104n
Tom Green County, 30

trestles, 14, 15, 27, 31, 61, 62, 85, 97
Trinity and Sabine Railway, 77–78
Trinity County, 80, 81
Trinity River, 4, 15, 21, 46, 72
Trinity River bridge, 62
Trinity, Texas, 73, 74, 75, 77, 78, 112n
"Turnips and New Onions," 89
Tweed, Charles H., 65
Tyler Tap Railroad, 82
Tyler County, 18
Tyler, Texas, 11, 17, 22, 82, 84

Union Trust Company, New York, 20, 27, 36, 43, 60, 61
Urbana, Texas, 15

Vair, Texas, 81
de Valernes, Viscountess, 9, 37
Van Alstyne, Mary E., 9
Van Alstyne, William A., 6, 7, 9
Vanderbilt, Cornelius, 2
Vanderbilt, William H., 2
Victoria, Texas, 103n
Virginia (The), 6
Vreeland, Texas, 73

Wabash, 94
Waco, Beaumont, Trinity and Sabine Railway, 73, 74, 78
Waco, Texas, 11, 16, 17, 74, 78
Wakefield, Texas, 21
Walker County, 75
Webb County, 30
Weldon, Texas, 74, 75
West Coast, 73, 94
West Texas, 30, 73
Western Narrow Gauge Railroad, 21, 104n, 105n
Western Union Telegraph Company, 64
"We Won't Be Back Till Saturday," 73
White City, Texas, 84
White Rock, Texas, 77
Wiener, Eli, 112n
Willard, Texas, 78, 79 (photo)
William Carlisle and Company, 73
Williams, J. W., 45
W. I. Watson (The), 6
"Wobblety, Bobblety, Turnover and Stop," 73
Woden, Texas, 89
Wofford, Mrs. C. D., 45
Wood County, 18
Woodbridge, G. G., 44
"Wooden Axle Road." (*See* Texas and New Orleans Railroad.)
Woods, W. E., 13, 15, 19
Woody, W. A., 45

Yoakum, R. D., 44

Zimmer, J. C., 9
Zimmer, Kate. (*See* Kate Bremond.)